SHORTCUTS
TO DECORATING
COUNTRY STYLE

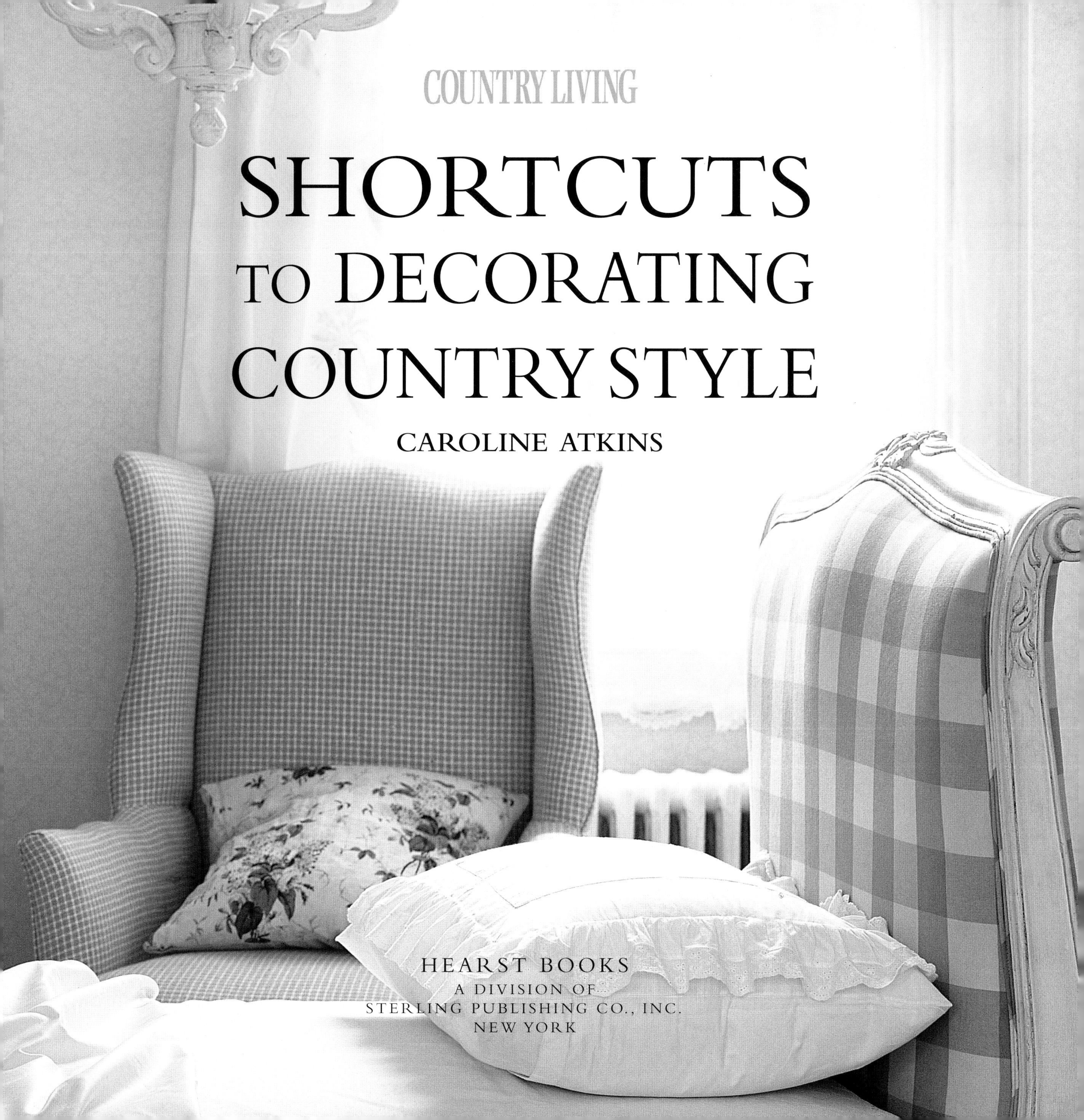

COUNTRY LIVING

SHORTCUTS
TO DECORATING
COUNTRY STYLE

CAROLINE ATKINS

HEARST BOOKS

A DIVISION OF
STERLING PUBLISHING CO., INC.
NEW YORK

Library of Congress Cataloging-in-Publication Data

Atkins, Caroline.
  Shortcuts to decorating country style / Caroline Atkins.
      p. cm.
Includes bibliographical references and index.
  ISBN 1-58816-285-0
  1. Decoration and ornament, Rustic. 2. Interior decoration. I.
Title.
  NK1986.R8A87 2004
  747--dc22

                                    2003021692

Published by Hearst Books
A Division of Sterling Publishing Co., Inc.
387 Park Avenue South, New York, NY 10016

Country Living is a trademark owned by Hearst Magazines Property, Inc.,
in USA, and Hearst Communications, Inc., in Canada. Hearst Books is a
trademark owned by Hearst Communications, Inc.

www.countryliving.com

Distributed in Canada by Sterling Publishing
c/o Canadian Manda Group,
One Atlantic Avenue,
Suite 105 Toronto,
Ontario,
Canada M6K 3E7

Project Editor: Serena Webb
Copy Editor: Gillian Haslam
Designer: Christine Wood

Reproduction by Classicscan Pte Ltd.
Printed and bound for Imago in China.
This book was typeset using Bembo and Frutiger.

CONTENTS

FOREWORD by Nancy Mernit Soriano

Editor in Chief of *Country Living* Magazine

If there's one thing we could all use it's more time to devote to the people we love and the things we love to do. But since squeezing extra hours into a single day is simply not possible, our only viable solution is to incorporate time-saving techniques into our busy lives. That's where *Country Living Shortcuts to Decorating Country Style* can be a great help, and I'm confident it will be as welcome an addition to your home as it's been to mine.

On these pages you'll find more than 500 tips and tricks for every room in the house—not only the living room, kitchen, and bedrooms but hallways, landings, and home office as well. Some are projects you can spend a weekend on, some require an afternoon's attention, and some take mere minutes to complete. (One of my favorites was the transformation of ordinary shoeboxes into stylish storage by covering them with beautiful fabric or paper.) Best of all, even though the ideas in this book are "shortcuts," the resulting looks are anything but rushed. Each one exudes the same relaxed country charm that we feature in Country Living month after month. Guests will wonder where you found the time!

Think of a classic country kitchen, and an image of a traditional range cooker comes to mind. Here botanical prints in simple wooden frames decorate the arched recess housing such a stove, with freshly harvested garden produce awaiting the cook's arrival.

INTRODUCTION

The essence of the country is its unhurried pace, a quality that characterizes country decorating as well as everyday life. Gentle colors, mellow wood, faded fabrics, and natural stone create a sense of timeless style in country homes, giving the impression of buildings and furnishings that have been there for ever. But for all their established quality, such distinctive country elements as these needn't take an age to acquire. Certain colors and features act as touchstones for country style, evoking traditions and images that transport you to a time and place of more tranquil mood. This book uses those touchstones to devise more than 500 shortcuts, suggesting individual tricks and treatments that will bring the country to life throughout your home.

Some are instant ideas—a combination of flowers perfect for a hall table, a paint color that will transform a sitting room, a fabric that gives a window a completely new look. Others are quick projects that teach the reader traditional country crafts. Throughout the book there are quick-reference panels highlighting the fastest, simplest decorating ideas: classic kitchen color schemes; bedroom fabrics that conjure up instant country style; accessories to frame in a seaside-style bathroom; easy place settings for a country dining table. Each chapter focuses on a different area of the house, and a final chapter provides a treasure trove of decorating ingredients that you will find invaluable for quick projects in any room.

Mellow wood furniture, simple ceramics, worn brickwork, and rough-plastered walls combine to establish an instant sense of country living, which responds beautifully to natural sunlight and needs just a handful of fresh garden flowers to bring it to life.

CHAPTER ONE

Living Rooms

As the room that is most on show, the living room needs to please everyone, adapting to

different moods and purposes throughout the day. This chapter helps you achieve the perfect

blend of function and elegance, with quick ideas for choosing the right colors, versatile

lighting, and elegant accessories, and for improvising additional furniture when it's needed.

The best living rooms have an indefinable sense of natural style that invites you in and makes

you feel effortlessly at home. Furniture is selected and arranged with welcoming informality.

Cushions and covers contribute extra layers of comfort, and their mixed fabrics cast a pattern

of gentle color over the whole room. The key to this look is a sense of calmness and

relaxation. It's an effect that relies more on feel than on appearance, so trust your instincts

and let the room find its own natural stillness.

COLORS AND PATTERNS

1 Adaptable colors

Living room colors need to be gentle and mellow in order to provide a tranquil background for relaxing throughout the day. They must also be adaptable to different pursuits and times, so among the most versatile are soft creams and nearly-neutrals, such as taupe and oatmeal. Warm, buttery shades will take the chill off a north-facing room, while cool slate blues and grays will soothe a space that gets ample sun. All these tones will reflect a natural country palette, adding distinctive character without overwhelming the room with color.

2 Layered fabrics

It's not always easy to find a single fabric design that suits the room all year round, especially if your home is subject to big changes in the amount of light it admits. One solution is to have a selection of different drapes that reflect the mood of the space at different times of year. Crisp cottons and sheer, floaty voiles are perfect for summer, while heavier velvets, chenilles, and tapestry fabrics will keep the room warm and welcoming in chilly winter months. For the in-between seasons, try layering several fabrics together, adding as many as you need for the required effect.

SIMPLE COLOR SCHEMES FOR COUNTRY LIVING ROOMS

● *Blue and white* Classically elegant with a comfortable freshness. The color of traditional tea sets such as Spode and Willow Pattern, and perfect for fabrics in checks, florals, or *toile de Jouy*.

● *Green and lavender* Hazy and romantic, with a natural beauty. An incredibly restful combination, good for subtle mixes of fabrics and paint colors.

● *Sweet-pea pastels* Pretty shades reminiscent of summer gardens. Combine cushions in a random mix of pinks, blues, mauves, and creams, or set a pale pink armchair against a soft lilac wall.

● *Coral and cream* Rich and indulgent, but very tranquil. Cream is perfect for paintwork and carpets, while warm, flame-tinged pinks make welcoming furnishings and add graceful accents.

● *Red and white* For Scandinavian simplicity. If the contrast feels too stark to be used in quantity, try it in small details like gingham curtains and cushions, or a single checked chair beside the fire. ◄

Red and white linen slipcovers conjure up an instant sense of Nordic simplicity in country living rooms.

3 Broken paintwork ▶

Rough-plastered and broken-
paintwork effects have a casual, slightly
worn appeal that makes the room feel
well-used and durable—reassuring you
that the practicality of the space is more
important than a perfect finish. This look
works especially well on uneven walls, as it
creates interesting areas of light and shade
and disguises imperfections that would be
highlighted by a flat coat of color. To
achieve a simple color wash, use a good
latex paint as a primer, then dilute your
main color (about 1 part paint to 5–8 parts
water, depending on how strong you want
the color), and brush it quickly onto the
primed surface, varying the direction of
your strokes. Keep brushing without
reloading the brush, so you work the paint
into a soft glaze. When the first coat is dry,
apply another using the same technique—
this time in a slightly darker shade so the
surface appears to have more depth, and so
the lighter color shows through, giving the
whole wall a glowing, translucent look.

*Color washed paintwork, with one shade layered over
another in a "drift" of strokes, creates a translucent
effect and gives the wall more depth.*

4 **Painted floorboards**

As an alternative to carpet, a painted floor will provide the perfect background for rugs and matting. Specialist floor paints are available in a wide range of colors, but soft white always looks clean and fresh and will leave you free to change your furnishing colors as often as you want. Clean your floorboards well and paint them according to the paint manufacturer's instructions, or give them a couple of coats of matte latex paint and seal with several layers of clear matte varnish.

5 **Household linens** ▶

Functional household fabrics more often found in the kitchen or the garden shed can give a fresh, crisp look to furnishings in other rooms. Plain white kitchen linens banded with primary colors, tough striped mattress ticking, coarse cream muslin, and loose-woven burlap (rather like the sort used for garden sacking)—all these can be commandeered for use as chair and

Household ticking and simple stripes will add a fresh, utility look to armchairs and sofas.

sofa slipcovers. If smaller items, such as dish towels, don't provide enough fabric for practical use, stitch them together patchwork-style into larger lengths.

6 **Loose slipcovers** ▶

Loose slipcovers have a practical, informal quality that keeps living room furniture comfortable and welcoming. Whether they're made from old-fashioned country-house chintzes or simpler, workaday stripes and checks, the effect is of materials intended to be used and reused, instead of kept for best—rather like an apron designed to withstand everyday wear before being cleaned and put back to work. Basic slipcovers are easy to cut for most chair styles, and contrasting winter and summer fabrics will allow you to change the look to suit different seasons.

Right: Removable slipcovers create an everyday, usable feeling, making a room look practical and hard-wearing.

COUNTRY MOTIFS FOR FABRICS AND PAPERS

● **Birds** Plump, colorful birds conjuring up a country garden setting. Perfect for covering fireside chairs and making comfortable cushions.

● **Leaves** Fresh green oak leaves, gentle willow fronds, or autumn patterns in russet and gold. Combine them with plain fabrics in toning colors, use them for drapes, and enjoy them alongside natural accessories such as beachcombing and hedgerow finds.

● **Feathers** Creating floating, gauzy patterns that work particularly well on sheer fabrics such as voile

or organza, but will also provide a subtle wallpaper background. They can be embroidered as individual motifs onto plain cottons and linens.

● **Berries** Crisp and colorful, clusters of summer strawberries, raspberries, and red currants, as well as the traditional winter berries of holly and rowan, add a fresh, lively look to drapes, cushions, and neat-patterned wallpapers.

● **Rosebuds** The classic country cottage pattern, strewn with dainty floral sprigs to suit smaller rooms, and easy to pair with checks and stripes. ▶

7 Mixed patterns ▼

A mixture of patterns gives the room a more welcoming, less formal feel than a setting where everything is perfectly coordinated. The secret is to find a common color that links the different designs, so the effect isn't totally random but has a unifying theme. Floral fabrics in contrasting patterns and scales will blend as naturally as the blooms in a garden border if you look for shades that echo and complement one another, while a color-schemed combination of plains, florals, and geometric motifs such as stars, stripes, or checks will add more interest to the mix.

8 Contrasting colors

If you feel daunted by mixing patterns, keep to a single design idea but let different colors give the room vitality. Flowers in various shades will mix comfortably, and plains and simpler patterns will offset one another effectively if you introduce clever contrasts. Stripes and checks will work well in contrasting primary colors such as reds and blues, conjuring up a practical, school-room look. Solid colors accent each other beautifully: cover armchairs in ice-cream pastels, or add russet and gold cushions to a denim-blue sofa, so the primary blue is brought to life by a complementary orange.

FURNITURE

9 Informal seating

Mix different styles of seating for a relaxed setting that conjures up effortless country style. Avoid the strict formality of matching sofas and three-piece suites and opt instead for a comfortable combination of individual chairs in different shapes and sizes, from rounded little tub chairs to elegant wing-backs, with the occasional low footstool or ottoman to vary the levels. A squashy sofa or two mixed in among such a casual arrangement will appear far more welcoming than if displayed as a formal centerpiece.

10 Daybeds and chaise longues ▶

If a full-size sofa feels too bulky for a cottage-style room, improvise with alternatives such as chaise longues and daybeds. The classic chaise longue design always looks elegant and less obtrusive, because it has a low back and a single arm —also often quite low—giving a sweeping, streamlined effect that takes up less room. Wooden-framed daybeds are especially practical if you want to provide extra sleeping space for occasional guests, as they will sit flat against the wall like a divan bed (with an elegant arm at either end creating the equivalent of a head and footboard) and can be stacked with cushions to provide a comfortable backrest.

For a country-style living room, avoid a totally coordinated look, and combine different patterns and furniture to create a more relaxed, informal setting with a genuinely welcoming feel.

Right: A daybed or chaise longue, with ends that fold down into a bed shape, offers more flexibility than a traditional rigid sofa design.

11 Painted furniture ◄

Pale, painted furniture has a pretty, fresh style that combines well with plain wood, lightening the overall effect. China cabinets, bookcases, writing desks, and little upright chairs will all benefit from this treatment. Choose pale shades that blend with the room's color scheme, and use eggshell paint which has just enough sheen to be practical and washable, but hasn't the institutional glare of high gloss.

12 Benches and windowseats

Built-in bench seats fitted into window recesses and alcoves make the most of your space for relaxing and entertaining, supplementing existing chairs and helping to define the shape of the room by outlining its architectural features. For added comfort, create long, flat cushions by cutting lengths of thick seating foam to fit the recess, then sew simple box covers. Measure all six cushion sides—including the "depth" of the foam—then cut panels of fabric accordingly, adding a little extra all around to allow for seams. Stitch them together right sides facing, leaving one of the edges open, then turn them right way out. Add a zipper, snap fasteners, or hook-and-eye fastenings to the open edge, and slot the cushions inside.

13 Flexible arrangements

Keep the furniture flexible so you can change the setting for different seasons or occasions. The most successful country

White-painted furniture often suits the soft color schemes found in country-style living rooms.

living rooms have an indefinable sense of welcome, inviting you in and making you feel naturally at home, and this is best achieved when they are easily adaptable. Seating positioned around the fire in winter can be moved into a sunnier, more open arrangement during summer months, and it's useful to keep a supply of additional chairs (folding garden chairs are perfect) for extra guests.

14 Contrasting wood tones

Mix different woods in varying colors to bring a richness of tone to the living room. Gauge the effect of the different finishes and combine them as you would any other palette, to create complementary contrasts and gentle highlights. The mellow gold of oak, pine, and cherry is warm and autumnal. Mahogany and rosewood add deep, dramatic purply browns. And pale woods like ash and beech add a creamy lightness that can be enhanced with bleaching or liming effects. (For an instant alternative on inexpensive junk-store finds, paint with a coat of diluted white latex, leave to dry, then sand down so streaks of white remain in the grain).

15 Blanket boxes

Wooden trunks and blanket boxes offer the double benefit of storage inside and display or table surfaces on top. Position one between two sofas to act as a coffee table, and you'll also provide yourself with a useful place to store magazines and newspapers, and to tidy away the personal possessions that invariably start to colonize a family living room.

ACCESSORIES

16 Hand-trimmed cushions ▼

Pretty cushions are essential to the comfort of any living room, and the simplest designs will make chairs and sofas far more inviting. Decorate a plain linen or muslin cushion with a single embroidered lace handkerchief stitched on to create a diamond pattern, or with a sprinkling of tiny satin ribbon rosettes. Or make your own covers from scratch. This is a great way to use up leftover scraps from other furnishing projects, by stitching them into patchwork-style cushion covers. Old woolens can be recycled, too: machine-launder them on a hot cycle to "felt" the wool so it toughens and mats and won't fray when cut. For daintier, more elegant designs, use lengths of satin or organza ribbon, stitching them together in bands to create a delicate pleated effect, or weaving them through one another at right angles so they form a checkered pattern.

Ribbon ties and embroidered detailing will finish plain cushions in decorative style, to make sofas and armchairs even more inviting.

DETAILS THAT ADD INSTANT COUNTRY STYLE

● *Pleats* The carefully folded pleats and pintucks that trimmed the bodices of old-fashioned cotton nightdresses will add a neat finish to fabric accessories such as cushions and lampshades. Either starch the tiny folds for a crisp finish, or leave them free to soften and ruffle slightly.

● *Rope* Plain hemp looks simple and practical, and also has a slightly nautical feel. Use it as an alternative to silk cord for edging plain linen cushions, or to tie curtains to their rod, or to bind a lampbase.

● *Buttons* These add dainty definition wherever you use them. Look out for interesting colors and finishes, and build up a stock of fabric-covered, glass, painted, and mother-of-pearl buttons that can be stitched along curtain edges or used to fasten cushion openings.

● *Toggles* In wood or horn, these add a more interesting fastening for cushions and curtain tiebacks. Attach loops made from cord or fabric to the opposite edge to complete the fastening.

● *Tassels* Colored silks and soft linen cord tied in a chunky knot with trailing ends are extremely tactile. As well as using them as curtain tiebacks, stitch them to cushion corners for a touch of luxury, or hang them from key handles to make them decorative as well as functional.

● *Braid* Wavy rickrack, embroidered ribbon, and twisted cord will all add distinctive edging to covers, throws, cushions, and curtains. Hunt out interesting designs in notions stores and always keep remnants left over from other furnishing projects.

17 Samplers and tapestries
Old-fashioned stitchwork combines beautifully with faded country living rooms. The detail of the pattern intrigues the eye and creates a focus of interest on cushions and chair covers. This is also a way to introduce a variety of additional colors without overwhelming the room, because such tiny quantities are involved. Look for tapestry or petit-point seat covers (or make your own using pre-designed kits), turn embroidered tray cloths into lightweight cushion covers, and frame hand-stitched samplers to hang on the wall.

18 Basket storage ▼
Use open containers such as baskets and trays for living room storage. One of the pleasures of country style is its comfortable, unstructured feel, which manages to present an attractive face to the world without having every last element of clutter hidden away behind closed doors. Instead, books, china, glassware, and personal treasures on open shelves become part of the furnishings. Baskets will hold everything from fireplace logs and kindling to letters, magazines, and sewing paraphernalia—and tidy away essentials such as keys and television remote controls.

19 Covered files and boxes ▼
If you don't trust yourself to keep clutter from spoiling the overall effect of the room, stock up on pretty files and boxes to store letters, bills, and other "pending" correspondence neatly on a shelf. Files covered in fabric or decorative paper and tied with ribbon will make it far easier for you to deal with paperwork efficiently, and won't look too office like for a relaxing living room.

Traditional woven baskets are the perfect portable way to store sewing and knitting equipment without hiding it away.

Files and boxes covered in pretty fabric or paper will keep correspondence and paperwork neatly filed yet close at hand.

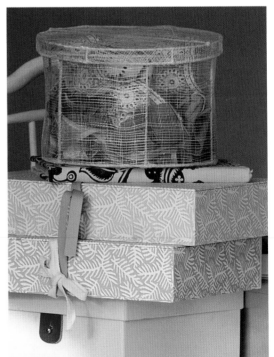

20 Gadget hideaways

High-tech gadgets such as televisions and sound systems aren't really part of the country decorating tradition, so look for furniture that will disguise modern gadgetry or help it to blend into the background. Site the equipment in traditional-style cupboards so you can close the doors on it when it's not in use. Invest in elegant storage racks to "file" your CDs, videos, and DVDs along with your books, or slot them into wicker basket trays that can slide in and out of your shelves like drawers.

21 Displaying china ▶

Put your china on show and let the intricate patterns and delicate glazes add their own color and style. Think of plates as alternative pictures, and create a wall display that groups them intriguingly above a mantelshelf or in an alcove. Choose designs that work well together and work out your arrangement before hanging them by laying them out on the floor. Alternatively, cut brown paper templates to the same size and stick them on the wall with reusable putty adhesive to try them out in different positions and groupings.

Open shelves allow you to keep your favorite china platters and dishes on show so they can double as display items, rather than being hidden in a cabinet.

22 Homemade papier-mâché

Traditional schoolroom crafts make instantly evocative use of country treasures and nature finds. Collect leaves and flower heads to press, and rediscover the childhood pleasure of making papier-mâché dishes and vases. Using a kitchen basin as a dish mold, dip strips of thin paper in white craft glue mixed with an equal amount of water, and apply them to the basin, gradually building up translucent layers of paper around it. Add your pressed decorations before the final layer; then, when the paper has dried, gently ease the papier-mâché dish away from the basin inside it.

23 Fresh-cut flowers ◄

Keep flower arrangements as relaxed as possible, choosing a natural look rather than anything too elaborate. Use fresh blooms cut from your own yard, or, if you are buying flowers, try a massed display of a single type. The simplicity of shape and color will make a real impact, rather than individual flowers trying to fight for your attention. Tulips, daisies, narcissi, and scented hyacinths are all perfect for country living rooms. (Remove any lower leaves to keep the arrangement fresh longer, and replace the water in the vase every few days).

Scented lilac blooms in soft shades of pink and mauve will fill your living room with gentle color and a pleasing fragrance.

24 Pressed and dried blooms ◄

Dried flowers have lost some favor in recent years, acquiring a slightly fusty image due in part perhaps to the amount of dust the flower heads themselves tend to gather. But drying and preserving flowers is still an excellent way of providing your home with natural decoration and dainty details that can be incorporated into other accessories (such as papier-mâché items, as described on the opposite page), as well as scented oils and potpourri. To press flowers, place them between sheets of paper, slot them between the pages of a heavy book, and weight down well to increase the pressing effect until they are dried and flattened. To dry fresh flowers such as roses while preserving their shape, tie them securely in bunches and hang upside down in a warm, dry place for two weeks. This treatment also works extremely well for lavender, which will last longer in arrangements if dried first. For potpourri, use old-fashioned scented flowers such as roses, stocks, lavender, carnations, and violets.

Hang bunches of lavender upside down to dry them, then use in arrangements, or add the flowers to bowls of scented potpourri.

QUICK FLOWER ARRANGEMENTS FOR COUNTRY LIVING ROOMS

● *Mixed anemones* These simple blooms have their own natural drama, the slim stems and softness of the petals contrasting with those brave pinks, reds, and purples, and startling black centers. Like roses, they look good in all stages of unfurling, from closed and secretive to tattered and fading.

● *Grasses and seed coats* These make an intriguing alternative to traditional blooms once floral color has died down in the garden. Try ornamental grasses such as miscanthus or stipa, or giant hogweed for more dramatic effects. Stand them in tall glasses and display in a window so light filters through stems and plays on the softer fronds.

● *Roses and sweetpeas* Gather small posies of short-stemmed flowers to add beautiful scent and soft, relaxed blooms to a side table or windowsill.

Plunge them into cold water as soon as they're cut, then arrange in pretty china such as a floral teacup or sugar bowl.

● *Hydrangea bowls* The big mop-heads and feathery lacecaps of old-fashioned hydrangeas create clouds of gentle color when displayed in a shallow bowl. Cut them in early morning, when conditions are cool and damp. If the heads start to wilt, immerse the stems in hot water to revive them.

● *Snowdrop posies* You can use lilies-of-the-valley for this effect, too, cutting the stems short and bunching them in tiny containers such as cream jugs or old-fashioned desktop inkwells. Add plenty of greenery as a background to accentuate the delicate shape of the flowers—use dark ivy leaves if you need extra foliage. ►

25 Picture effects

Paintings need to provide overall impact as well as individual interest, so try them out in different arrangements before you decide on your hanging positions. Grouping them together will help to "lift" any weaker images and turn undistinguished paintings into an interesting collection. You can see the effect by experimenting with a set of simple botanical prints or architectural drawings that, individually, appear rather dry and academic, but acquire a comforting, schoolroom-style symmetry when grouped together in a block or line.

26 Single images ▶

Bear in mind that the more distinctive the image, the less attention you need to draw to it. A single gem of an oil painting will have a nonchalant, understated sense of occasion if simply propped on a table, chest, or mantelshelf, leaning against a wall or standing in an alcove. The element of surprise is always important, and a good picture positioned subtly in the shadows will have more drama (and run less risk of dominating the room) than if given pride of place and lit for deliberate effect.

A single painting propped casually on a mantelshelf is conveniently displayed at eye level so that it can be appreciated more easily.

27 Informal displays ▶
    Don't assume that your pictures should create formal exhibitions; the most effective displays are relaxed and natural, with the framed images treated as part of the furnishings rather than objects of reverence. Aim to keep them around eye level, so you can appreciate them easily as you pass through the room—or try a gallery-style display by smothering an entire wall with random pictures in different media and on different subjects, so that no single image stands out and the whole collection simply creates an intriguing backdrop for other furnishings.

28 Family photographs
    Old family photographs are the perfect images for a relaxing living room, conjuring up a sense of personal history and turning walls and shelves into a gallery for significant characters and memories. A collection of photos of different sizes and heights, casually overlapping one another on a shelf or mantelpiece, can provide layers of interest, giving the viewer glimpses of family history.

This random grouping of different images and styles helps to create an informal focus of interest on a living room wall.

WINDOWS

29 **Shutters and sashes**
Some windows are beautiful enough to need barely any dressing. Tall, well-proportioned sashes and French windows opening onto a garden or terrace may be better off without drapes or curtains, so their elegant lines can be seen to best effect. Check whether the original shutters are still in place, and let their simplicity offset the window's architecture, or fit new ones to frame and define it.

30 **Dried-leaf designs** ◄
Use the intriguing shapes of different fall leaves to make autumnal headings for plain muslin or linen curtains. Dry a selection of striking shapes, complete with their stems, then spray-varnish them to protect and strengthen them, so they don't crumble away on handling. Hang them upside down and attach them by their stems to the curtain top with curtain clips, so they create a golden frieze against the window.

The distinctive shapes and colors of dried leaves create a striking look when clipped to the top of a muslin curtain.

Cobalt-blue gingham curtains trimmed with a fuchsia-pink fringe are decorated with a cluster of matching pansies tucked into a velvet ribbon tieback.

CURTAIN DETAILS FOR COUNTRY LIVING ROOMS

● *Ribbon tops* Use short lengths of colored ribbon to tie lightweight voile or muslin panels onto the rod.

● *Portière rods* Fit simple gathered curtains onto hinged metal brackets that will fold across the window like shutters.

● *Button-throughs* Layer two contrasting fabrics to create a detachable lining, by fixing buttons along the top of one and making matching buttonholes in the other.

● *Grommet holes* Punch a row of grommets along the top of the curtain and thread the rod through them, or lash it on with nautical-style cord.

● *Instant valances* Fold the top of the curtain over to create a deep valance before fixing to the rod or wire with decorative clips.

LIGHTING

31 **Flickering candlelight** ▶
Use the beauty of natural candlelight to add sparkle and vitality to nighttime living rooms. Even if the main source of illumination comes from electric lamps, carefully positioned lanterns and candelabra will contribute variety and atmosphere with their flickering glow, creating pools of light and interesting areas of contrast and shadow. Groups of candlesticks and simple chandeliers will cluster flames effectively together, while a single candle in a traditional storm lantern will cast a softened beam across the room.

Right: Fat pillar candles massed together on a dark wood mantelshelf echo the firelight and add instant warmth and atmosphere.

HOW TO CREATE ATMOSPHERIC LIGHTING

● *Crystal droplets* Rounded teardrops and crystal-cut faceted glass chips will both add instant charm to existing lamps. Hang them from the rim of the shade so that they catch the light and sparkle with vitality.

● *Paper lanterns* Make a simple cuboid base from lightweight modeling wood and glue, then stretch waxed translucent paper over it. Fit the paper around the frame, creasing it along the corners to mold it into shape, then use a scalpel or craft knife to cut a design into each side before attaching the shade to the frame with thin strips of double-sided tape. Stand the shade over a tealight or candle so the beam highlights the cut pattern. (Always be careful when using candles in paper lanterns.)

● *Cut-tin shades* Ready-made metal shades will create the same effect as paper lanterns, for use with either candles or electric light. Position the lamp where it casts the pattern of its cut-out design onto a floor or wall.

● *Sconces* Side lamps cast a gentler beam than central or overhead lighting, and wall-mounted candle sconces, with a reflected metal or mirrored backing to bounce light back into the room, are perfect for evening living rooms. ◀

CHAPTER TWO

Kitchens

Kitchens are above all practical, but the country kitchen has an enduring image as a place of warmth and welcome—a setting to enjoy as well as a functional workstation. This chapter shows you how to create that look with traditional colors and quick touches: the distinctive charm of blue-and-white china clustered randomly on hutch shelves; handwoven baskets co-opted for use as vegetable storage and flatware trays; a lineup of potted herbs to grow on the windowsill and sprinkle into your cooking. Well-designed kitchens have robust good looks that can withstand everyday use and a tough working regime, but their cabinets and fittings add decorative color as well as practical lines, and their most basic accessories can supply a neat finish that captures the essence of country style.

COLORS AND PATTERNS

1 Summer colors
Match the glow of old pine with warm paint colors in yellow and terra-cotta to conjure up a sense of the Mediterranean and give the impression that it's summer in your kitchen all year round. Chalky paint finishes will recreate the dry, powdery look of rough-plastered walls, and terra-cotta floor tiles are rich and sun-warmed.

2 Neat stripes ▼
Stripes have an air of neat, domestic precision that suits them perfectly to kitchen use. Practical and unassuming, they can be mixed in different weights and colors—wide against narrow, vertical against horizontal—and the simple stripes found in fabrics and wallpapers are easy to echo with banded ceramics such as Cornishware, and the clean lines of upright ladderback chairs around the kitchen table.

3 Colored tiles
Much of the color and pattern in the kitchen is supplied by the ceramic tiles used for splashbacks and worktops—and the texture of the glaze contributes its own character to the effect they create. Handmade tiles have a naturally uneven surface that catches the light, provides interesting variations in design or pigment, and gives each one a sense of individuality. Plain tiles with a more matte quality to the glaze add a rich, light-absorbent finish that is cool and calming.

Striped fabrics and banded china suit the neat, domestic simplicity of a traditional country kitchen.

COLOR SCHEMES FOR COUNTRY KITCHENS

● *Blue and yellow* Cheerful and sunny, a country-cottage scheme that gives the kitchen an all-day vitality. Aim for a soft, clear yellow background such as primrose—good for opening up small spaces—and add blue paint-work and accessories to bring the room to life.

● *Green and cream* The old-fashioned colors of the dairy and pantry, cool and restful and faintly reminiscent of the kitchen garden. Mix cream tiles and ceramics with apple green paintwork, and add old-fashioned cream enamelware with green lettering and details.

● *Red and blue* Fresh and stimulating with a slightly folk-art feel—think of Nordic style and New England patchworks. This works well with old pine furniture, as the crisp colors offset the mellow tones of the wood.

● *Cream and white* Soft and subtle, conjuring up the classic country-house look with a cool, rich combination, like whipped cream on lemon syllabub. Where plain white can be cold and stark and all-cream slightly cloying, layering the two shades together creates the perfect balance. Try cream china on a white hutch, or white-painted cabinets against gentle cream walls.

● *Blue and white* Inspired by the classic image of the kitchen hutch piled with chunky striped Cornishware. It's almost impossible to go wrong with this mix, so try different blues together, combining bright cornflower and deep navy among softer sky blues.

CLASSIC KITCHEN FABRICS

● *Striped ticking* Thick cotton striped with narrow lines of black and white or navy and white will make practical kitchen curtains and seat cushions. You may also find variations with the stripes in red or green.

● *Spotted cotton* Use a classic polka dot crisp cotton to make into dish towels and tablecloths and match it with hand-painted pottery. Mix contrasting colors such as blue spots on green, yellow spots on blue, and white spots on pink.

● *Cream calico* Natural, slightly rough-woven cotton with a clean, bright quality that instantly freshens up any room in which it's used.

● *Blue denim* Practical and utilitarian, the ideal working fabric with a touch of easy color thrown in for good measure. It somehow manages to forget its blueness and behave like a neutral shade, understated enough to mix effortlessly with other colors and patterns.

● *Natural linen* Soft oatmeal and stone shades that work beautifully with old-fashioned kitchen ceramics such as ironstone jugs and classic yellow-ware mixing bowls. Perfect for a dairy-style kitchen full of creams and whites.

● *Checked gingham* Bright and cheerful, in primary colors and white, with the scale varying from tiny checks to large squares. It's perfect for curtains, tablecloths and jelly jar covers. ▷

Mix different shades of blue on your kitchen shelves for a friendly, informal effect.

CABINET FRONTS WITH COUNTRY STYLE

● *Fabric fronts* Pretty material, either gathered on curtain wire at top and bottom or stretched and tacked onto battens inside the door, will provide pattern and color, and add a soft finish. You can use this technique with or without glass, or dispense with the door frame altogether and hang simple curtains beneath worktops to conceal shelves and kitchen appliances.

● *Glass panels* Glazed doors provide a lighter effect than solid wood, and let you display attractive china while keeping it dust-free. If you're not convinced your cabinets are tidy enough to put on show, use frosting spray or stick-on film to create frosted patterns and obscure the glass.

● *Drilled patterns* These can be used to decorate plain wood doors with whatever motifs you want. Work out a template on paper first, then transfer it onto the door and use a wide-gauge drill bit to follow the pattern with evenly spaced holes.

● *Cutout designs* Like drilled patterns, these need to be planned on paper first and positioned carefully. Keep them simple—folk-art style hearts or plain lozenge shapes—and use a jigsaw to cut them neatly and accurately.

● *Chicken-wire* This combines a sense of hard-working practicality with an attractive tracery of pattern, either used on its own to create a mesh across the door, or to provide a little robust protection for fabric panels. ◄

The combination of chicken-wire fronts and a wallpaper lining is very pretty in this kitchen cabinet.

FURNITURE AND FITTINGS

4 Shaker simplicity

Use the understated principles of traditional Shaker style to give your kitchen natural calm and practical elegance: clean furniture lines, plain paneled cabinets, muted earthy paint colors, and everything based on simple functionality, with no unnecessary fuss or ornament. Keep your high-tech gadgets out of sight so that the only utensils on show are basic hand tools such as knives and whisks, and look for storage containers in natural materials—wicker baskets and planked wooden trays. For space-saving practicality hang folding wooden chairs on a wall-mounted Shaker style peg-rail to keep them out of the way when not in use.

5 Tongue and groove ▶

Use painted tongue-and-groove wood paneling as a gentler alternative to ceramic tiles for worktop splashbacks, or panel a couple of walls to provide a mellow, beach-house look. The vertical lines of the planking will create neat stripes to help increase the sense of height in low-ceilinged rooms, and the whole effect feels practical and slightly nautical. It's also a clever way to conceal a less than perfect wall surface.

Tongue-and-groove paneling forms a neat splashback behind the sink and draining board.

6 Box shelves

Old fruit crates fixed securely to the wall create instant display shelves as an alternative to fitted wall shelves. Keep a special look out for crates with a cross panel dividing them into two sections, as this will provide an extra shelf if the crate is hung vertically. It doesn't matter if the base is open-slatted or rickety, as this will sit flat against the wall to form the back of the unit. Just make sure the sides and end pieces are sound, as these will become the shelves and need to take the weight of your china or cookery books. Paint the crate to match your kitchen color scheme, or leave it unfinished for a more rustic, artisan effect.

7 Traditional hutches ▶

The traditional design of the kitchen hutch is a country staple, ideal for both storing and displaying your tableware, cutlery, and linens, however they do take up a lot of space. If you haven't room for a full-size hutch or can't find a design you like, improvise your own version with a display rack or set of open shelves fixed to the wall above an old pine chest or table. You can adjust the position of the two pieces so they fit your space exactly, and paint them to make a matching pair. Marble-topped washstands make excellent bases, too, as the cool marble provides a useful worktop for rolling out pastry.

The open shelves of a freestanding hutch are the perfect place to display favorite kitchen china.

8 Painted chairs

Amid the mellow warmth of traditional old pine furniture, a few painted chairs will add fresh contrasts and lively color. Use a single color to create a matching set, or select shades from a palette that reflects the style of the kitchen. Try sugared-almond pinks, creams, greens, blues, and mauves against soft cream walls and with pretty floral fabrics, or experiment with earthy ocher, terra-cotta, olive green, and slate blue for a more muted, Shaker-style effect.

TRADITIONAL STORAGE IDEAS

● *Bicycle baskets* Old-fashioned bicycle carriers are usefully designed with one flat side that will hang neatly against a wall or on the inside of a cabinet door to hold anything from clothespins and utensils to vegetable supplies.

● *Overhead racks* Traditional racks raised and lowered on pulleys, are handy for hanging pans, cooking implements, and strings of onions and garlic. Hang individual items on butcher's hooks, adding extra hooks as needed.

● *Worktop containers* Use sturdy earthenware pitchers and jugs to keep utensils within easy reach. Wooden spoons, rolling pins, whisks, and so on can all be stored neatly on your worktop in this way.

● *Linen bags* Stitched from traditional kitchen linens or colorful cotton, with strong cord threaded through to create a drawstring neck, these are invaluable for storing essentials such as garbage bags, spare shopping bags, and clean dish towels.

● *Shallow trugs or baskets* More commonly found in the yard or the garden shed, these wide, woven-wood baskets will stand on the worktop, on the floor, or inside a cabinet to hold vegetables and other groceries.

● *Pegs and hooks* A row of simple hooks fixed to the wall or the underside of a wall cabinet will put colorful, shapely mugs on show, while wooden peg-rails provide practical places to hang sieves, pans, colanders, and so on. More decorative hooks can be used for individual items such as calendars and dish towels—look for appropriate kitchen designs such as silver cutlery bent into hook shapes. ▶

9 Freestanding furniture

One of the classic symbols of the country kitchen, freestanding furniture epitomizes a simplicity of style that relies on the beauty of individual pieces rather than sleek, fitted, high-tech convenience. The easiest way to "loosen up" a run of fitted units is to add a separate butcher's block or trolley, letting you adjust the layout of the room as you want, as well as providing an extra work surface. The most useful of these are fitted with wheels, making them easy to move, and have shelves or drawers for storage underneath.

10 Cooking ranges ▶

Nothing establishes the impression of a country kitchen as quickly as an old-fashioned cooking range. Solid and homely, a source of warmth and comfort as well as traditional home-baked meals, these cast-iron ovens provide a perfect centerpiece among the basketware and painted furniture. For a really mellow effect, look for an Aga cooker enameled in classic cream or soft duck-egg blue. Or opt for a cheerful fire-truck red, a classic dark green, or a rich, deep burgundy.

11 Classic sinks ◀

The deep, square design of the classic ceramic sink has a natural place in traditional country kitchens, especially when flanked by draining boards. Invaluable for trimming and arranging flowers, as well as for preparing vegetables and tackling family-sized loads of dirty dishes, these solid, slightly clinical-looking ceramic troughs provide an appropriate work center for the room Mrs. Beeton described as "the great laboratory of every household." Small-scale models are available to fit neater spaces and cottage kitchens. Pair your sink with traditional-style faucets.

Left: Equip your country-style kitchen with a classic, roomy ceramic sink.
Right: A pale blue Aga cooker creates a timeless kitchen centerpiece.

STORAGE

12 Plate racks

Old-fashioned wooden plate racks do double duty as drainers and storage, and are especially useful in small kitchens where space is at a premium. Fix the rack above your sink to make use of otherwise wasted space—it will provide an additional, temporary shelf for newly washed china and glassware before they are transferred to their usual home.

13 Pretty linings

Flatware drawers and cabinet shelves feel neater and more ordered if they are lined with sheets of attractive paper. Save wallpaper scraps so you have a stock of designs to choose from, or use commercial cabinet liner paper. Choose colors that will sit well alongside one another and create decorative contrasts with the color of the cabinet doors and drawer fronts.

14 Spice drawers

There's always something fascinating about miniature versions of full-size furniture designs, which is what makes the tiny drawers of spice boxes and old-fashioned pharmacist's chests so appealing. Perfect for storing small ingredients such as herbs, spices, flavorings, and stock cubes, which tend to got lost in larger drawers or pushed to the back of cabinets, they have a traditional farmhouse feel and the neatness of classic Shaker style. On a larger scale, multidrawered pharmacist's chests also make a good alternative hutch base (see tip 7 on page 36).

Use practical kitchen containers to hold simple arrangements of fresh garden flowers.

TOOLS AND TABLEWARE

15 Instant flower holders ◀
Practical kitchen containers make intriguing alternatives to conventional vases for displays of flowers and foliage. Requisition items like milk-jugs, coffeepots, and storage jars to hold simple blooms on the table or hutch top. Use sugar bowls and egg cups for tiny spring posies to decorate a breakfast tray. And create floor-standing arrangements of rushes and grasses in tall milk churns or pitchers.

16 Decorative enamelware
Put painted enamelware on display alongside your china and glass to create the orderly calm of an old-fashioned larder. Traditional containers are often decorated with simple lettering to identify their intended contents, while jugs, mugs, and coffeepots can be found in more ornamental patterns, from bands and checkers to delicate floral designs. (Line enamelware with plastic if using to store foodstuffs, as chips in the enamel may rust).

17 Mixed china ▶
Kitchen crockery needs to combine the functional with the aesthetic. Mixing different styles of china on shelves and hutches reinforces the idea that practicality is paramount, and your kitchen is equipped for all purposes, from family breakfasts to birthday celebrations and other special occasions. Chunky earthenware and multicolored spongeware will provide for everyday meals, and will sit comfortably next to intricately cut creamware and pretty floral chintzware.

Mix different styles of china on hutch shelves, from robust earthenware to hand-painted porcelain.

18 **Wooden utensils** ▶
Traditional utensils with a smooth, well-worn finish are pleasant to use and exude a natural sense of domestic history. The much-used handles of wooden spoons and rolling pins are comforting to find in a drawer or standing in a worktop pitcher, while the mellow grain of breadboards and butter molds has the timeless appeal of the farmhouse kitchen.

19 **Wirework and tinware**
Look out for interesting shapes and silhouettes that make functional items worthy of display. Rounded jelly molds, deep-bowled ladles, fluted brioche tins, and pierced tin graters all create distinctive outlines against a plain wall. Hang metal cookie cutters in different patterns as little decorations, or fix them to lengths of thread or thin wire and hang them from a frame as a ceiling mobile. The traditional spiral-wired kitchen whisk is just one of many wirework designs in intriguing shapes—from vegetable baskets and toasting forks, to trivets and plate racks.

20 **Hand-painted pottery**
Include a few hand-painted pieces among your kitchen china, creating your own designs to reflect personal themes and favorite recipes. Try out your ideas on paper first to practice them, then transfer them onto plain white china. Some ceramic paint can be used on glazed china, but this will need to be kept for display use only. Other techniques let you work on blank unglazed china or "bisqueware" (available from specialist ceramic and craft suppliers), painting your design in ceramic

Well-worn wooden spoons, spatulas, ladles, and rolling pins are comfortable to use and bring an instant sense of country style to any kitchen.

underglaze or applying "printed" patterns with a sponge or vegetable stamp. These will then need to be fired to fix the patterns and make the china usable. Look out for pottery shops, which will supply the materials, then glaze and fire your ceramics

for you. Painted designs of flowers, fruits, and vegetables will suit a country kitchen, or you could opt for simple stripes and spots. Alternatively, add decorative lettering identifying the owner of the piece or its intended use.

DETAILS AND ACCESSORIES

21 Pretty fabrics

Even the most functional items can be chosen to coordinate with your furnishing scheme. Look for pretty fabrics or vintage florals to make essential kitchen linens such as dish towels, oven cloths, and ironing board covers, so that they are a pleasure to use and make chores feel less like hard work.

22 Pictures and paintings

For all their functional practicality, the best kitchens provide a comfortable environment in which to be in during the day and therefore benefit from some of the ornament and decoration you'd expect to find in a sitting room. Paintings will make the space feel more homey and lived-in. Look for simple still-lifes with a comforting, domestic appeal, such as images of fruits, vegetables, and crockery, and make the most of home-grown talent by framing children's pictures to hang on the wall or pegging them to a clothes line strung across the ceiling.

23 Cushions and seat pads

Add a selection of cushions for color and comfort, and to take the edge off hard kitchen chairs. Match them to other linens such as aprons and ironing board covers, or look for colors and patterns that pick up the designs on your tableware. Tie-on cushions (little flat seatpads made with ribbons in the corners to let you attach them to the chairbacks) will be less likely to go astray when chairs are moved around.

24 Cheesecloth food covers ▼

Even in our amply equipped times of fridges and cooler boxes, there's a simple charm to the traditional cheesecloth covers that were once routinely used to protect milk jugs, cake plates, and other food containers from dust, insects, and birds. To make your own, use small square or circular panels of cheesecloth or linen (table napkins are an ideal size) and stitch colored beads or shells to the corners or around the edges to act as weights.

25 Homemade preserves

Bottle the colors of each season by making your own preserves, jellies, and flavored oils and vinegars, so their translucent reds, golds, and oranges glow with goodness when lined up along a pantry shelf. Even if the fruits themselves aren't homegrown, there's a delicious pleasure in the making and flavoring of individual preserves, either for your own use, or to give as gifts.

A natural linen food cover weighted with shells around the edges is a traditional sight on jugs and bowls in a cool country larder.

26 **Food on show**
Take a lead from traditional farmhouse kitchens and keep larder provisions on show to make the most of their natural good looks. Display vegetables in dishes and on platters as you would fresh fruit—squashes, aubergines, and purply red onions add glossy color and distinctive shapes, and painted metal colanders make good impromptu fruit bowls. Hang bright red chilies where their color catches the light, and enjoy the smooth curves of fresh eggs displayed in a dish or on a stand. (For the best effect, look out for wonderful free-range eggs with shells in pastel blues, greens, pinks, and yellows).

27 **Shelf trims**
To give plain kitchen shelves a more decorative look, pin lengths of lace or embroidered ribbon or braid along the front edges. Choose colors and patterns that match or contrast with the china on the shelves. More robust trims can be added with lengths of lightweight medium-density fiberboard cut into gentle scallops or pennant points. Create a paper template for the pattern, then mark it on the wood in pencil, and follow the lines with a jigsaw. Where the shelves are recessed into an alcove, fixing the shaped wood across the top will create a pelmet effect and give them a neater finish.

28 **Colorful pot covers** ▶
Save fabric scraps left over from furnishing and dressmaking projects to make decorative lids for jellies, preserves, and chutneys, cutting the fabric into neat circles with pinking shears to prevent the edges from fraying. Tie them over the pot lids with matching ribbon, or with garden twine or natural raffia for a simpler effect, and add labels identifying the contents. You may find luggage-style labels tied to the necks of the pots more practical than papers stuck directly onto the glass, as they are easier to remove and replace when the pots are used for different produce the following year.

KITCHEN BASICS TO KEEP AND RECYCLE

● *Bottles* Look out for interesting shapes and colors to reuse for homemade oils and vinegars, or just to display against a window and hold the occasional long-stemmed flower. Traditional spring-stoppered bottles are especially useful as they make airtight containers for homemade ginger beer and lemonade.

● *Cookie tins (and other food containers)* A brief trawl through a fleamarket or junk store will prove how collectable old tins have become, so start searching for interesting designs to make antiques of the future. Use them to store freezer bags, labels, and other kitchen essentials.

● *Food labels* Wine labels, orange papers, and other colorful food wrappers (particularly foreign labels brought home from travels abroad) provide an intriguing touch in a kitchen. Display them in a simple wooden frame hung on the wall, or use them to cover small storage boxes and recipe files in a decoupage-style collage.

● *Jars and tumblers* Functional glassware can be recycled and used for homemade preserves and chutneys, or decorated with painted designs and recycled as simple flower vases.

● *Fruit crates* Stack these wooden crates against the wall and label them to store vegetables and other provisions if you're short of conventional cabinet space, or to sort bottles, newspapers, and other kitchen refuse in preparation for the next garbage collection.

Cotton fabrics left over from other sewing projects can be used to make cheerful pot covers.

29 Message and reminder boards
Children's blackboards requisitioned for shopping lists, messages, and reminders give the kitchen a nostalgic, schoolroom feel, evoking memories of mid-morning milk and chocolate cookies. Keep different colored chalks for different types of shopping—fresh food, pantry supplies, and other essentials—or for messages aimed at different members of the household. Use the board for reminders of school events, dental appointments, vacation dates, birthdays, and so on. Keep a cloth handy for cleaning it.

HERBS TO GROW ON YOUR KITCHEN WINDOWSILL

For sunny sills:

● *Chives* Long slender leaves, like a lighter-weight version of scallions, that can be cut and sprinkled over pale soups, scrambled eggs, and salads for a crisp, fresh flavor.

● *Basil* Delicious with tomatoes and soft cheeses, and perfect for use in sauces, soups, salads, and pasta dishes. Water if the leaves start to droop.

● *Nasturtium* A herb for the windowbox on the outer sill, with both flowers and leaves providing instant garnish. Add the hot, peppery leaves to salads and soups, scatter the fresh orange yellow flowers over a salad, or use crystallized petals as cake decorations.

● *Thyme* A familiar flavor from traditional stuffings, and generally good with meat and game, this will benefit from sun and aridity to concentrate its taste.

● *Rosemary* Snip off aromatic sprigs to cook with lamb or mix into stuffings for strongly flavored meat and game. Use in moderation, and remove the sprigs before serving.

For shady sills:

● *Parsley* The curly variety is a classic garnish, and goes beautifully with fish, bacon, and vegetable dishes.

● *Mint* Keep a pot of spearmint to cut for mint sauce and jellies, and to flavor new potatoes and garden peas.

● *Chervil* The leaves look a little like parsley. The subtle flavor can either be used on its own with eggs and fish, or it makes a good blend with other herbs (such as the *fines herbes* mixture used for traditional French omelets).

Notes:
To encourage fresh young growth and to keep the plants flourishing, pick the leaves regularly and don't let them flower (apart from nasturtiums, see left).

Sun-loving herb plants shouldn't be overwatered; just keep the soil slightly moist (but watch out for basil, whose leaves can droop very suddenly if it dries out). Shade-happy plants are best stood in a tray of gravel so that they stay moist but drain well and don't become waterlogged.

30 Simple curtains and shades ▶
Keep kitchen windows as simple as possible to avoid unnecessary fabric getting in the way of worktops and appliances. Roller and Roman shades are the neatest of all, worked with a basic cord-and-cleat mechanism that adds a practical, nautical-style feel. For small windows where simplicity is paramount, half-length café curtains, covering just the lower part of the window, or gathered valances that trim the top without screening much of the glass, are a good alternative to avoid obstructing already limited light. Use crisp, lightweight fabrics in small-scale patterns or simple stripes and checks to keep the effect fresh and neat. Traditional linen dish towels can be transformed into simple gathered curtains to match the function of the room and avoid frills or fuss. Use a matching pair of dish towels, turning over the top edge to make a narrow channel for the curtain wire, or just attach them to the wire with a row of metal clips.

A simple valance will screen the top of the kitchen window without obscuring light or getting in the way of your worktop.

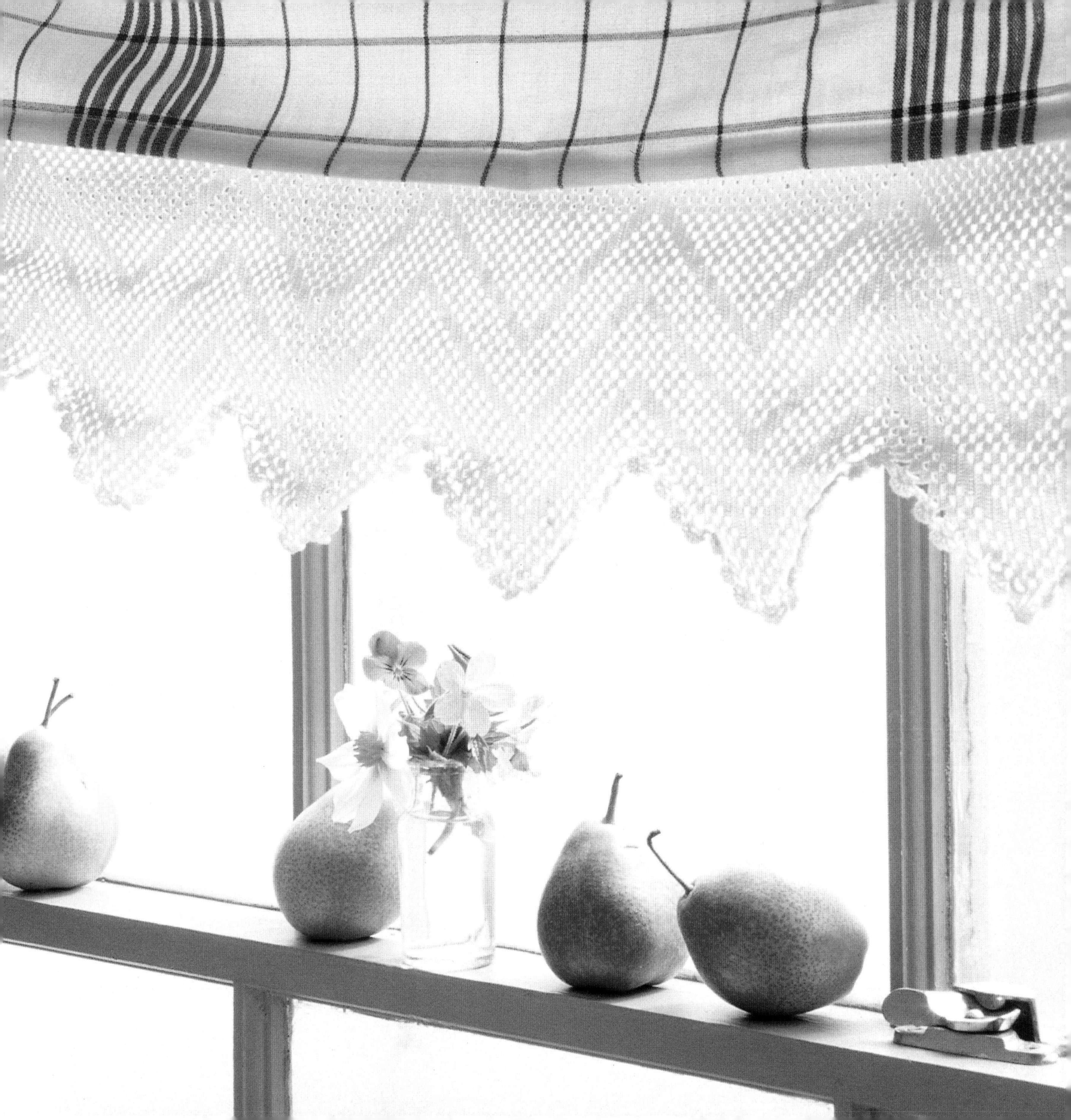

CHAPTER THREE

Dining Rooms

Dining rooms need to be the most adaptable of rooms, achieving a complete personality change from everyday family meals to special occasions and formal celebrations. Simple furnishing ideas will help them switch roles more easily. Use different styles of china to establish the right atmosphere for each event. Keep a stock of different linens to set the table with contrasting effects, and add natural candlelight to make the setting glow with mellow warmth or sparkle with lively celebration. Table decorations are the quickest of all trimmings to achieve. Trails of greenery and vases of fresh-cut flowers add instant ornament to a plain cloth, and a spray of herbs or an ivy-circled napkin will turn an empty plate into a country place setting. The trick is to stay relaxed and not aim for too much formality. Well-chosen pieces of individual beauty will have more impact than total coordination.

COLORS AND PATTERNS

1 Curtains ◄
Celebrate the subtle ease with which
different china designs mix on your
shelves by using the same principle to
make patchwork curtains. Collect fabric
remnants in colors and patterns to match
your china, then stitch them together in
neat panels, interspersing plain sections
to offset the more elaborate weaves and
prints. Make blue and white curtains to
match classic china such as traditional
Willow Pattern and Asiatic Pheasant.
Use simple stripes and plain linens in
conjunction with neutral earthenware and
banded slipware, and pick pretty sprigged
cottons to echo the delicate florals of
traditional chintzware.

2 Architectural details
Use decorative moldings and
architectural details to give the room a
sense of natural elegance, following its lines
without adding any forced ornament. Even
plain unpaneled doors can acquire their
own distinction: paint or paper them to
match the rest of the walls and, if the room
has a dado rail, continue this across the
door too, so that it turns into one of those
"secret" doors sometimes seen in stately
homes and country houses.

*Patchwork curtains will echo the different colors and
patterns of mixed china designs and create a homely,
welcoming scene.*

3 **Decorative wall plaques** ▶
Use offcuts of decorative wood molding to make painted wall plaques featuring traditional plasterwork patterns. Isolate individual sections of the design—such as a fleur-de-lis, rosette, or egg-and-dart motif—and glue each one onto a panel of medium-density fiberboard cut to size. Paint the whole plaque with latex or eggshell in natural shades to represent stone or slate, or in soft pastels to add a hint of gentle color, and fix it to the wall or stand it on a mantelshelf or display shelf.

Decorative moldings, fixed to wood panels and then painted, create classical-style wall plaques. Either attach to the wall or display on a shelf.

TIMELESS DINING ROOM COLORS

● *Glowing yellow* Take inspiration from natural sources and paint the walls in Mediterranean ocher or the slightly softer shades of cornfields and haybales. Partner it with warm yellow pine and add touches of gold for accent and definition, such as gold-patterned china and gilded picture and mirror frames.

● *Warm red* From orangey terra-cotta to bright scarlet and deep wine red, this is a glorious palette for dramatic dining room effects. Add dark polished wood and leather for a sense of traditional luxury, and set the table with classic white linen and china, adding plenty of crystal and glass to catch the candlelight for extra sparkle.

● *Shaker blue-green* Look for a muted, indefinable shade that isn't quite one color or the other—and yet somehow isn't turquoise either. This should be a restful, understated shade that mixes beautifully with natural earthenware pottery, and also provides a subtle background for china and fabrics in more definite colors, such as blues, pinks, and yellows.

● *Rich cream* Mellow and buttery, this has the warmth of yellow but a quieter, less dramatic character. Incredibly versatile, it will blend beautifully with the pinks and greens of floral china, the classic blues of Wedgwood and chinoiserie, and the chunky glazes of simple kitchen-style tableware.

● *Soft stone* Somewhere between gray and cream, this puttylike shade is wonderfully adaptable, good for creating more contemporary country effects as well as providing the perfect backdrop for traditional furniture. Try it with plain china and neutral linen-covered chairs, for a simple look that is elegant but understated, adding natural foliage and grasses for decoration.

● *Classic white* Go for soft or antique white rather than the starkest bright shades, and you can evoke any style from beach-house or cottage to faded country-house grandeur. It looks particularly good on paneled walls, and when hung with plenty of framed pictures.

CLASSIC LOOKS FOR COUNTRY DINING ROOMS

● *Rustic farmhouse* Combine the mellow tones of old pine furniture and chunky natural earthenware with table displays of harvest-style fruit bowls and wall-hung wreaths woven from dried grasses and hedgerow finds. Good for casual entertaining.

● *Gustavian elegance* Choose painted furniture in graceful shapes and pale, light-reflective grays, blues, greens, and creams matching them with cool silver and pewter accessories, elegant white or cream china, and simple table linen in muted checks. A versatile setting easily adaptable from casual to formal meals.

● *Vintage floral* Go over the top with fabrics in a whole garden-full of flowers, from fat 1950s cabbage roses to tiny cottage sprigs. Set the table with densely patterned chintzware and Victorian floral porcelain, and add bowls of soft-petaled roses and peonies to complete the effect. Perfect for summer teas and lunches.

● *Simple beach house* Mix plain, fresh colors against a painted tongue-and-groove background. Set a basic trestle table with simple tableware and picnicware in bright ceramics, adding unbreakable acrylic plates and tumblers for practical family lunches. A relaxed setting for any time of day.

● *Faded glamor* Create a sense of drama with lots of crystal–pressed or engraved glassware, glass-handled flatware, a chandelier over the table, and crystal droplets hung from candles and vases. Look for faience-style tableware in pretty shapes and pastel colors with an antiqued glaze for a classic French look. For elegant lunches or romantic dinners. ◀

Crystal and lace add a sense of faded glamor to this elegant table setting.

4 *Trompe-l'oeil* china

Supplement a display of traditional china on the dining room wall by painting additional plate patterns directly onto the wall surface, creating elegant designs that blend beautifully with the real thing. Simple hand-painted ceramics are relatively easy to imitate freehand, as long as you give yourself an accurate outline by tracing around the actual plate. More complex designs can be achieved with specialist stencils, cut to mimic the intricate motifs of classic porcelain.

5 Selecting your shades

Choose decorating shades that suit the time of day when the room will be used most often. Bright primaries are fresh and invigorating for breakfasts and everyday lunches; soft, sweet shades will complement elegant tea services and delicate iced cakes; and rich, dramatic colors create a striking background for evening meals and formal dinners. For a dining room that is likely to be in use at any time of day, aim for warm, glowing colors that will respond well to both daylight and candlelight.

6 Checkerboard floors

Painted floors can create a host of different effects underfoot in country dining rooms. Plain white or cream painted boards have a simple, artisan feel. To add an elegant checkerboard effect, similar to a traditional tiled floor, start with a base coat of white, then use a tape-measure and pencil to mark out your squares, defining them with masking tape to give a clean edge. Paint alternate squares in a contrasting color and wait until it has dried before removing the tape. Smart checkers become comfortable country plaids if you mix in a few extra colors and add occasional careful stripes and lines as well as the neatly defined squares. And decorative borders can be added around the edges of the room, either worked freehand or using stencil templates. If you are concerned about comfort and noise underfoot, add a rug to soften the effect.

7 Contrasting metals ◄

Enjoy the varying tones and finishes of different kinds of metalware, mixing them together in your table settings so that their contrasting colors add depth and luster to the table. The reflective shine of silver looks all the more festive against the dull gunmetal gleam of pewter. Gold and gilded accessories are warmer and richer, and the brightness of simple tin lanterns adds a clean, fresh note.

A silver-painted candlestick adds a touch of sparkle beside the gentler gleam of a pewter teapot.

FURNITURE

8 **Instant seating** ◄
Requisition a few folding slatted chairs from the garden or summerhouse to provide extra seating for parties and family get-togethers. Their painted wood colors will mix easily with country dining furniture, the addition of pretty cushions will keep them comfortable, and you can decorate the backs with little wreaths or posies (see Quick Tricks to Give Your Chairs Country Style, opposite).

9 **Mix-and-match furniture**
Don't worry about everything having to match: the most welcoming dining rooms mix different wood tones and include elements of painted furniture too. The most important thing, in a room where people will be sitting in one position for a couple of hours at a time, is comfort. Make sure the chairs are supplied with cushions if necessary, and that the table is high enough for knees to fit comfortably underneath.

10 **Cafeteria-style benches**
Keep the setting friendly and informal by replacing chairs with cafeteria-style benches for sociable suppers. Set one on either side of a long table, topped with seat pads or with a single flat box cushion filled with thick foam cut to fit the bench. You'll be able to fit more people around the table, and the atmosphere will be far more relaxed and convivial.

Folding garden chairs—with the addition of seat cushions for comfort—will supplement your dining room seating.

QUICK TRICKS TO GIVE YOUR CHAIRS COUNTRY STYLE

● **Country colors** Paint them with a coat of eggshell paint (or for a quick-drying version, use latex then wax or varnish the surface to protect the finish). Turn mismatching junk-store finds into a matching set, or give an existing set individual style by painting each one a different color.

● **Fabric covers** Make simple slipcovers in linen, gingham, or sprigged cotton, cutting basic panels to fit the seat and back, and four individual drops around the legs. Stitch each cover right sides together, leaving the leg panels open (just turning the edges to neaten them), then turn it the right way out and drop it over the chair. You can add pretty ribbon ties to knot the seat edges loosely at each corner.

● **Floral touches** Decorate chairbacks with little bunches of tied flowers or hang a miniature wreath on each one. This creates a delicate effect for special occasions, and guests can take their own posy or wreath home as a gift.

● **Gilded highlights** Accent the shape of the chair, and any decorative carving, by using touches of gilding cream, gold paint, or metal leaf to create rubbed-gold highlights and give an antique effect.

● **Pretty cushions** Add tie-on cushions to echo the paint colors. Fix ribbons or fabric ties to the corners and loop these around the legs to keep the pad in place. ▶

Fabric slipcovers can match your chairs to your table linen, or just add some extra color and decoration to the scheme.

11 **Display shelves and plate rails** ▶
Keep favorite china on show on sideboards and plate racks, so that its colors and patterns can be enjoyed throughout the day, not just on special occasions. Look for purpose-built racks that hold plates in place behind a rail, with a groove or ridge into which the rim can slot to prevent it from slipping. Or line them up on a high-level display shelf around the room, or create groups of selected patterns fixed to the wall with adhesive pads or elastic grips.

12 **Corner shelves**
For additional storage, fit rustic shelves into an unused corner of the room, to keep plates and glasses close at hand without taking up wall space or making an overt display of them. Cut sections of plain unfinished wood into chunky wedge shapes, each one large enough to take a stack of plates in the angle where two walls meet, and fix to the wall with brackets.

13 **Mirror images**
Turn a small breakfast room into an ornate dining room, fit for any occasion, by adding a huge gilded mirror on one wall. It doesn't need to be hung or fixed in place, so you could make it a temporary arrangement by borrowing a decorative mirror from a bedroom. Just leaning against the wall, it will have the desired effect of reflecting the light, doubling the size of the room, and establishing a rich, convivial setting—and will have all the more impact for its casual, nonchalant style.

Old-fashioned china on pretty paper-lined shelves makes an elegant display.

CHINA AND TABLE SETTINGS

14 **Old-fashioned china** ▼
Enjoy the elegance of traditional china on special occasions: graceful cake stands with tiers of delicate china fixed to a silver centerpiece always look wonderful at a celebration. Deep-bowled tureens and long-handled ladles are perfect for spooning out soups and sauces, and a raised pedestal dish can hold a display of fruit.

Traditional tableware such as this delicate raised pedestal dish will give a dining table an instant, timeless elegance.

15 **Layered settings** ▼
Take a relaxed attitude to your tableware and don't attempt to make everything match. It's far more interesting and enjoyable to mix different designs together—plains among patterns, one color offset against another. Layer and alternate pieces from different sets so they create a new collection each time you use them, combining floral patterns with checks, or plain white with bright ceramics in other colors, or florals in different shades and scales. You could even buy several sets of

Pretty china in different colors and patterns can be mixed in various combinations to let you "design" new sets for yourself.

the same design in contrasting colors, and then have fun mixing them up so that the shapes match but the colors always surprise and intrigue.

16 **Everyday ceramics**
Incorporate functional kitchen containers into informal dining table settings. Use mixing bowls to serve soups and vegetables, keep colored enamel colanders to hold displays of fresh fruit, and offer little pudding basins as individual soup bowls, cereal dishes, or grapefruit dishes.

17 **Bright picnicware**
Mix bright plastic and acrylic picnicware among hand-painted ceramics for everyday lunches and suppers. The combination of plain primary colors and simply patterned earthenware has a fresh, lively feel that suits family dining rooms and colorful painted furniture. Add plain cotton table linen, and save colored glass mineral-water bottles to use as carafes and flower holders.

18 **Colored glass** ▶
Glassware in different colors will dress the table in a whole rainbow of contrasting shades, but its translucent quality manages to unite the different hues so they complement one another rather than clashing. Simple tumblers, elegant cut crystal, and individually designed dishes and vases will add their own impact. Make sure the table is well lit with candles and side lamps to catch the colors and keep them glowing.

Colored glass will catch the light and cast beautiful rays onto a white tablecloth. Use colored tumblers to serve water or to hold a few long-stemmed flowers picked from the garden.

COUNTRY-STYLE PLACE SETTINGS

● *Stacked plates* Give your guests an immediate indication of how many courses there will be right from the start. Pile up a stack of plates and dishes to be worked through in layers, with a name card on top marking each place.

● *Little gifts* Lay a crisp linen napkin on each place, with a piece of fruit or a bag of candies on top as a gift.

● *Fresh herbs* Place a spray of ribbon-tied greenery or a sprig of fresh rosemary on top of each folded napkin before putting on the plates.

● *Cutlery boxes* Pack each guest's cutlery in a little gift box beside their plate, so that they are each treated to a flash of silver when they open it.

● *Individual posies* Tie posies of flowers and stand one in a little vase at each place as presents for your guests.

● *Wrapped cutlery* Wrap each guest's cutlery in a traditional linen napkin or dish towel, to recreate the timeless feel of a French country café. ▶

Traditional linen napkins and sprays of fresh herbs help to conjure up a rustic French atmosphere.

QUICK NAPKIN RINGS

● *Wire twists* Fine fuse wire looks as delicate as jewelry when threaded with colored beads. Wind the wire around the napkin so that it forms a sort of bracelet, with the beaded decoration sitting on top. Or thread a single bead onto a short length of wire and twist this around a plain wire "bracelet" to hold the strands in place.

● *Raffia ties* Simple linen or plain cotton napkins can be loosely tied with natural-colored raffia. Finish in a bow or knot, and fray out the ends so they start to "tassel."

● *Flowers and feathers* Pick plumage and petals that match the colors of your tableware, then slip a couple of feathers under a simple ribbon-tie napkin ring, or use fine wire to hold delicate flower heads (these can be real, fabric, or paper) in place. ▼

● *Identity tags* Tie the napkin with ribbon, cord, or thick string, and add a luggage label inscribed with the guest's name as a place marker.

● *Ribbons and bows* Use narrow satin ribbon, wound round several times then tied into a bow. Or look for wired ribbon, which will form a relatively stiff ring and can be twisted into a rosette for a final flourish.

● *Woven foliage* Wind sprays of ivy around each napkin, or use tiny-leaved greenery such as box or cotoneaster and twist it around thin wire so that it can be shaped into the guest's initial.

● *Buttoned cuffs* Cut a length of wide ribbon, or hem a strip of linen, to about 6inches (15cm) long, then stitch a button onto one end and make a matching buttonhole in the other, so the fabric can be buttoned around the napkin to hold it. ▼

Left: A narrow velvet ribbon and a spray of feathers trim this elegant white napkin.
Above: Simple buttoned cuffs create a neat, contemporary look.
Right: Tiny silk rosebuds on fine wire stems can be wound around napkins to form a "garland" effect.

19 **Country table linens** ▶
The fabric you use on your table makes all the difference to the style of your dining room. Classic white linen—usually in the form of subtly woven damask patterns—is the ideal background for china and glass and will match any color scheme effortlessly. A simpler effect can be achieved by using plain linen sheets (don't worry too much about pressing them to perfection— the rough-dried effect has a robust country charm). Dainty printed cottons, such as paisleys and florals, have a neat, French provincial look about them, while colorful checks and stripes always feel practical and welcoming.

20 **Edible treats**
Decorate the table with traditional treats so that it becomes an irresistible centerpiece. Arrange little dishes of sugared almonds, gold and silver dragées, sugar-dusted Turkish delight, or chocolate-dipped fruits between the serving dishes, or add a handful to each guest's plate as a place setting. Sprinkle more dragées and sugared almonds on the tablecloth (this needs to be plain white linen or damask for the best effect) for a real sense of luxury.

Pretty, colored embroidery and neat bands of ribbon give plain white table linen a softer, less formal look.

FLOWERS AND LIGHTING

21 Natural decorations

Don't reserve table decorations only for Christmas. Celebration meals at any time of year, especially at nighttime, will benefit from many of the elements that make Christmas settings so atmospheric, such as candlelight, scent, and greenery. Surround candles with deep red roses and bundles of cinnamon, or set the table with autumnal bowls of nuts, fir cones, and seed coats. In spring, use a small vase of cheerful miniature daffodils as a centerpiece. For summer dining tables, include dishes of smooth pebbles and coral-colored shells, fresh and cool and reminiscent of beach walks and open spaces.

22 Flowers and foliage

Trail fresh greenery and flowers across the table, letting it lie between the dishes and swagging it around the edges like a daisy chain. Ivy is one of the most compliant plants, being abundantly leaved without thorns or prickles, and able to lie flat so its clear leaf shapes form distinctive silhouettes against a white cloth. In summer, you can achieve the same effect with sprays of freshly cut jasmine, its white buds adding delicious scent as well as delicate pink-tinged color against the glossy leaves.

23 Tealights, tapers, and candles ▶

Set the table with flickering candlelight to bring the setting to life with a peaceful glow. Decorate fat pillar candles with circlets of beads, crystals, and greenery and stand them in clusters of different heights so their flames reflect and multiply one another. Stand clusters of slim tapers in bowls or pitchers (anchor them securely in a layer of sand), and make use of little Oriental-style tealights, too, placing them on decorative plates or floating them in bowls of water so the flames move together and apart in a slow dance.

Candles of different sizes and heights will reflect each other's glow, creating a sparkling atmosphere.

24 Crystal-droplet chandeliers

Keep the lighting soft and atmospheric, adding sparkle and creating shadows rather than bathing the whole dining room in an equal level of illumination. Hang a chandelier over the table to diffuse the light and accent your tableware and decorations; real candles are unbeatable, but tiny candle-shaped bulbs in an elegantly designed electric chandelier will have the same gentle effect. Supplement this with side lamps and sconces around the edge of the room to make guests feel enclosed and protected.

25 Christmas tree lights

Use strings of tiny white lights to create extra sparkle for special occasions. Dig out your Christmas decorations and hang them along the front of the mantelshelf, catching them at intervals so that they form gentle scallop shapes. Or swag them around the table itself, twining them with greenery so they twinkle on the glossy leaves against the crisp white background of the cloth.

26 Crystallized flowers

Give tea cakes a traditional finish by sprinkling them with old-fashioned flowers. Rose petals, narcissus heads, pansies, primroses, and violets will all add a touch of delicate nostalgia. To crystallize fresh violets, paint the flowers carefully with egg white (beaten until just frothy), then dust with superfine sugar. Do a few at a time so you can sugar them before the egg dries. Leave to dry on baking parchment in an airing cupboard, on top of a stove, or in a very low-heat oven.

QUICK FLOWER ARRANGEMENTS FOR COUNTRY TABLES

● *Classic berries* Let the bright glow and bead-like shimmer of berries provide glossy details against plain linen. Holly, rowan, and hypericum add dramatic reds and oranges, while pale mistletoe and snowberries have a softer, subtler gleam.

● *Muscari posies* Gather the tiny blue spikes and slim stems of grape hyacinths into little posies, arrange in dainty bud vases, and stand one beside each place setting. Keep a few flowers in reserve to scatter across a plain white tablecloth and around the edge of pretty cake plates.

● *Floral fruit bowls* Mix the heady scent of stephanotis flowers with the fresh citrus of an orange bowl. A single trail of stephanotis will twine its white starburst blooms and glossy dark leaves elegantly among the glowing fruit.

● *Single blooms* Stand individual flowers in slim vases—one at each place setting or arranged in a row down the center of the table. Pick flower heads with distinctive outlines and stems strong enough to support themselves alone.

● *Blossom sprays* Arrange these in a pitcher as an alternative to traditional cut-flower displays, picking the fresh pinks and whites of fruit trees in early spring or the faded mauves and glorious scent of summer lilac.

● *Floating hydrangeas* Use hydrangeas so that the blooms are soft and full. Cut the stems short and float two or three flower heads, with a few leaves still attached, in a shallow glass bowl so that they turn gently and catch the light. ▶

A bowl of floating hydrangea heads provides an elegant table centerpiece.

CHAPTER FOUR

Bedrooms

Bedrooms are all too often decorated on the one-note theme of providing somewhere restful

and comfortable to sleep. But they also need to be refreshing to wake up to; they may supply

personal daytime space for reading or working; and they involve a fair amount of practical

planning to accommodate the necessary storage space for clothes and other personal

possessions—especially if you're fitting out a child's room. This chapter has ideas for bedrooms

in all their guises, suggesting restful patterns for fabrics and wallpapers, gentle colors to

encourage sleep as well as inspiring the room's daytime use, clever closet and shelving

solutions to keep things in order, and folding screens to divide children's rooms or cordon off a

dressing area. Whether your taste is for a simple, dormitory-style room with a plain metal bed

frame and hand-stitched quilts, or a romantic affair trimmed with lace and damask, it's the

finishing touches that will establish your style.

COLORS AND PATTERNS

1 Restful designs
Choose patterns to suit the scale of the room and to maintain a restful, calming air conducive to sleep and relaxation. Don't try to mix too many different designs or the effect will become frantic and unharmonious. If you are concerned that your pattern will dominate the scheme, limit wallpaper to a single wall or to the recesses on either side of a chimneypiece.

2 Metalwork and painted wood ◄
Avoid the slightly deadening effect that can result from too much dark wood in a single room by incorporating decorative metalwork (see Classic Country Bed Styles, page 69) and by including a few pieces of painted furniture among your dressing tables and closets. Bedside cabinets, bookshelves, mirror frames, and bedheads can all be painted in restful shades and a soft eggshell finish to coordinate with the colors of your walls and fabrics.

3 Light and luster
Country bedrooms should be havens of peace and romance. Take full advantage of elements that will effortlessly combine the two elements, such as iridescent silk and satin fabrics, lustered china and cut-glass crystal decoration. Light the room with droplet-hung chandeliers and sconces, and look for crystal-trimmed mirror and picture frames with faceted surfaces that will reflect and multiply the soft, low-level light.

Decorative metalwork and pretty bed linen add understated pattern to romantic country bedrooms.

CLASSIC COLOR SCHEMES

● *Sugared-almond shades* Deliciously edible, these soft pastels mix effortlessly together, creating washes of subtle color perfect for layering in bed linens, covers, cushions, and curtains.

● *Pink and green* Classic garden colors are always easy to use and these are particularly restful, balancing warm and cool tones and establishing a sweet, refreshing mix.

● *Stone and white* The ultimate in Zen-style relaxation, these neutral shades add a calming, contemplative sense of balance to country bedrooms. Don't feel cramped by the restricted scheme: be inspired by the decorative stitchwork of traditional white bed linen and nightwear, and set these against textured covers in stone-colored linen and restful walls painted in taupe or gray.

● *Lilac and blue* Fresh from the garden again, but also reminiscent of cooler, watery colors, these two overlapping shades are so close in tone that they simply enrich each other's crisp, refreshing qualities. Offset them with painted furniture in white or cream for the prettiest, daintiest look.

● *Blue and white* The combination of restful blue and crisp white is simple and classic. Use detailed *toile de Jouy* for an elegant French look, or stick to neat ginghams for traditional cottage style.

● *Faded cerise* Pinks of all kinds are natural bedroom colors, and the deeper tones add a sense of glamor, allowing you to experiment with more indulgent touches such as gilding and decorative metalwork, and the sensuous textures of satins and velvets. ◀

A crystal-trimmed mirror on a dressing table will sparkle in the sunlight, adding just a touch of old-fashioned elegance.

RESTFUL PATTERNS FOR FABRICS AND WALLPAPERS

● *Paisley* Flowers and leaves worked into a slightly abstract design, amid flame and teardrop shapes, will give a slightly Eastern overtone.

● *Single flower heads* Isolated blooms scattered across walls and bed linen create a very different effect than the more traditional floral designs. Often impressionist and freehand, they nevertheless have their own sense of drama, so the room needs only a few elegant pieces of furniture to add structure. Don't complicate things by adding more pattern.

● *Cottage sprigs* Traditional country-style rosebuds and blossoms in soft colors have a simple, nostalgic feel and are perfect for small bedrooms, where their neat patterns won't dominate or overwhelm the setting.

● *Bees* Think of honey and summer stillness, rather than industrious buzzing, and these classic emblems of sunny afternoons become a touchstone for quiet and calm. For the subtlest effect, look for bee motifs embroidered white-on-white across voile curtains and cotton pillowcases.

● *Butterflies* Their gossamer wings and delicate markings have a fragile beauty that works particularly well on shimmery organzas and silks, and somehow gives wallpaper the translucent quality of tissue or rice paper. Use butterfly designs sparingly, like precious gems, to line alcoves or cabinet doors, or to make delicately patterned shades for bedside lamps.

● *Stars* Create a night sky against your ceiling with gold or silver stars sprinkled against a soft background shade. Keep the stars small, as larger designs tend to evoke a more opulent, urban feel.

● *Toile de Jouy* These fanciful images of cherubs, shepherdesses, and pastoral scenes, worked in intricate detail and single colors against a white or cream background (traditionally red or blue, but also found in black, sepia, or brighter greens and yellow), are the stuff of dreams in romantic bedrooms. ◄

Ornate toile de Jouy elements such as cherubs and shepherdesses are very effective when combined with simpler country-style checks.

4 **Attics and eaves**
Make the most of sloping ceilings and interesting angles in attic bedrooms by highlighting their lines. Papering the walls in a printed pattern, or painting them in a different color from the ceiling, will create stronger contrasts, while beams can be painted for even more definition. Use the lowest roof space for a run of fitted closets, or position the bed here, where standing height is not so important.

5 **Simple headboards**
Plain wooden headboards are easy to transform with paint and fabric effects more in keeping with country bedrooms. Create a Scandinavian-style color scheme by painting the bedhead in soft grays, greens, or blues, continuing this finish onto other furniture to unify the look. Alternatively, fold a plaid rug over the frame, tying it at the sides with thick cord or attaching leather straps and buckles to fasten the edges more neatly. Or sew a simple fabric sleeve that can be dropped over the headboard to conceal it completely, adding beads and buttons for decoration.

CLASSIC COUNTRY BED STYLES

● *Decorative wrought iron* Ornamental ironwork provides intriguing patterns against the plain surfaces of walls and bed linen, with carved metal flowers, leaves, curlicues, and other flourishes twisting their way around the head and foot of the bed. Look for old painted frames as well as classic polished brass, and measure frames carefully when buying mattresses to fit them.

● *Platforms and box beds* Perfect for children's rooms, these can be built into an alcove so that they take up less floor space, or raised onto a platform with closets and storage beneath. They work just as well in adult rooms. Add little stools or library steps for access to higher beds, and—if you want the room to provide a play space or sitting room during the day—fit a curtain or door that can be folded across it to keep it hidden when not in use.

● *Sleigh beds and lits bateaux* These distinctive wooden frames, curving gently up at the head and foot like an elegant boat or a traditional carved sleigh, create a surround that holds the mattress firmly in place on all sides. Enjoy the traditional wood finish or, for a lighter, more cottagey effect, paint them in soft country colors.

● *Rustic woodwork* Plain wooden bed frames range from simple Shaker-style planking to upright Arts and Crafts designs faintly reminiscent of high-backed dining chairs. For a completely unique effect, commission a frame made from recycled lumber, complete with the scorch marks and nail holes authenticating its previous use and giving it a functional, artisan feel. This is a contemporary look that works well in simple whitewashed rooms, combined with plain cottons, linens, and calicos.

● *Dormitory-style metal frames* Simpler metalwork recreates the impression of a school dormitory, with plain barred end pieces to the beds and a slightly utilitarian feel that suits old-fashioned patchwork covers, cozy candlewick bedspreads, and thrift-conscious hand-knitted throws. ▼

Plain metal frames and simple striped linen conjure up an old-fashioned school dormitory look.

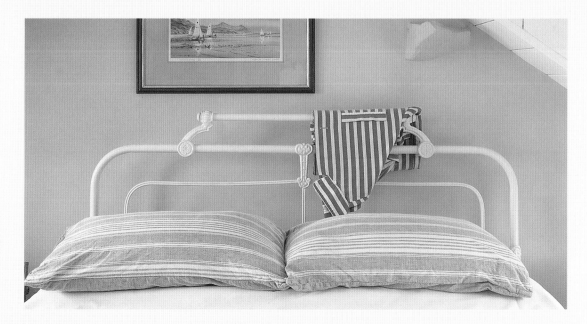

6 Flamboyant flourishes

The bedroom is one place where you can afford to go over the top and indulge yourself in flamboyant furnishings that might feel overpowering in daytime rooms. Living areas generally need to keep a lot of people happy from dawn till dusk, whereas bedrooms are private space into which others intrude only if invited. This is your chance to mix different patterns, decorate with whimsical colors of your own choice, and add personal flourishes that make the room feel your own.

7 Hand-painted images

As an alternative to the all-over designs of classic wallpaper, use individual stamped or stenciled motifs to create a drift of subtle pattern against a plain painted wall. Stencils have shaken off their slightly frantic, heavy-handed reputation and have reinvented themselves in a much gentler guise, while hand-printed images pressed lightly into place with a rubber stamp or individual woodcut will give a soft, feathery effect.

FURNITURE

8 Freestanding screens ◀

Decorated screens will divide off a corner of the room to provide a dressing area or work space, and can also be used to demarcate personal territory in a shared children's room. Blank medium-density fiberboard screen panels are available in a range of sizes ready for you to paint to your own design, or to cover with paper or fabric. Decorate the panels before hinging them together, joining three or four with hinges placed on alternate sides so they form a zigzag shape that allows the screen to stand unsupported.

9 Somewhere to sit

The best bedrooms are inviting during the day as well as restful at night. Adding an armchair will make the room feel welcoming, ensuring that it's a place to read or relax and seek a moment's refuge from a busy household. Even better, a chaise longue or daybed will provide the equivalent of a sofa—a comfortable place to sit, and an extra bed when needed for overnight guests.

A folding screen covered in elegant fabric will provide a dressing area in a traditional style.

10 **Armoires and linen presses ▼**
The beauty of old-fashioned
bedroom furniture is the way it combines
functional practicality with graceful design,
in the best traditions of country style. Such
simple elegance is timeless, and the classic
tall armoire and wide-shelved linen press
are still perfect for holding spare blankets,
linens, covers, and curtains, neatly folded
and scented with lavender or rose petals.

11 **Inspired improvisation**
The concept of simplicity that
underlies country furnishing depends more
on inspired improvisation than on the
more modern assumption that purpose-
designed furniture is available for every
situation. Thus a plain upright wooden
chair makes a neat bedside table, with
more sense of style and function than any
mass-produced cabinet.

DRESSING THE BED

● *White linen and lace* Combine
decorative lacework and embroidered white
cotton with fine plain linen sheets for classic,
cool romance.

● *Checks and stripes* Mix candy stripes and
bright gingham checks for children's rooms and
simple nautical effects, or look for woven plaids
introducing more complex bands of color and
creating a warmer, cozier feel.

● *Patchwork patterns* A random mixture
of cotton remnants in different colors and
patterns has a gentle, nostalgic quality that
sets the scene for a bedroom decorated with
homespun accessories and thrift-conscious
secondhand finds.

● *Traditional blankets* Old-fashioned knits
in practical earthy colors and occasional
unexpected pastels are appropriately simple and
functional for metal-framed dormitory-style
beds. Trimmed with an edging of plain blanket
stitch, they fold back over crisp sheets to give
a neat, tailored finish.

● *Satin eiderdowns* Use these to conjure
up a sense of classic luxury, picking shimmery
floral colors to match pretty pastel schemes,
or moody purples, pewter grays, and deep reds
for a more dramatic effect. The lustered finish
gives plain colors extra depth, and mixes
beautifully with old-fashioned patterns such
as toiles and chinoiserie.

*Neatly folded linens conjure up a classic picture of
domestic calm. Add sprigs of dried lavender to guard
against moths.*

12 Four-poster beds ◄

Opulent four-poster beds conjure up an unmatchable sense of romance, with their enclosing, territory-defining frame and drapes. Not every bed can be a four-poster, but a similar effect will be established if you add wooden uprights at the corner of a basic divan, creating a simpler, Shaker-style bedstead, or hang drapes or a canopy from a ceiling fixture. Use panels of heavy linen, corduroy, or tapestry fabric for a warm, enveloping feel, or go for a lighter, more romantic look with ready-made cheesecloth or voile curtains: gather them onto four single ceiling hooks fixed above the bed, and knot them loosely so they hang down to form fabric "pillars" at each corner.

13 Ornamental mirrors

Think of mirrors as light sources and ornaments as well as practical looking glasses in which to check your appearance. A single huge mirror in an ornate frame becomes a piece of furniture in its own right, while a whole wall of smaller mirrors, grouped like a display of paintings, will increase the amount of light and space, intensify the colors of your furnishings, create intriguing reflected images, and provide decoration in the individual shapes and styles of their frames.

DETAILS AND ACCESSORIES

14 Handles and doorknobs

In a room where mood is paramount and practical activity at a minimum, details are all-important in preserving the effect, and even functional fittings need to have an aesthetic appeal. Replace any door and cabinet handles that don't suit the style of the setting, looking for delicately fashioned cut-glass designs that will catch the light and add a jewel-like sense of luxury in plain crystal or opulent glowing colors.

15 Decorative lace

Frame fragments of decorative lace or panels of leftover fabric as an alternative to paintings and photographs. Look for deep box frames that will hold three-dimensional items, and use them to put personal treasures and favorite mementos on show—a child's christening gown or first pair of shoes, samplers and stitchwork celebrating special occasions such as weddings and anniversaries, theater programs, and vacation souvenirs, or simple hedgerow and beachcombing finds including shells, feathers, nuts, and leaves.

16 Laundry bags and lavender sachets ▼

Use leftover fabric from curtains and bed linen to make bedroom accessories, trimming plain linen with patterned borders or stitching patchwork patterns from fragments of different designs in coordinating colors. Larger pieces can be turned into laundry bags (stitch them around three sides and add a drawstring neck and cord around the fourth) and nightdress cases (again, stitch around three sides, but this time attach ties across one of the longer sides, or create an envelope-style flap that can be folded over and buttoned in place). Small pieces will make lavender sachets and potpourri pockets to slip among your clothes in chests of drawers and closets to ward off moths.

A traditional four-poster bed piled with soft pillows and cushions provides an instant sense of luxury and romance.

Leftover fabric remnants can easily be stitched into pretty laundry bags or used to make sachets for lavender and potpourri.

17 Wall hangings

Let wall hangings take the place of pictures, creating panels of color and pattern, with textural detail adding an extra layer of warmth against the flat surface behind. The beauty of a traditional patchwork quilt can be enjoyed all the more clearly like this. Middle Eastern kilims, their tough, flat-woven fabric originally designed to be used as curtains and traveling bags, have rich colors and intricate designs that will hang beautifully behind a bed to take the place of a conventional bedhead, rather like a medieval tapestry. And a single curtain will have much the same effect: look for ready-made tab-top panels, or fix a row of large rings along the top, and slot it onto a wall-fixed rod so it hangs like a banner.

18 Fresh scented flowers ◄

Stand jugs of freshly cut flowers on dressing tables and mantelshelves to scent the room and add simple garden color. Softly furled roses and peonies, pastel-colored sweet peas, frilly-edged pinks, tiny bells of lily-of-the-valley, and hazy sprays of lilac are all gently fragrant in restful bedroom shades. Use your prettiest china and borrow teacups and sugar bowls from the dining room for the smaller blooms and shorter stems.

The faded hazy colors of hydrangea flowers make a pretty display for a bedside table.

19 Pretty coat hangers

Even details as small as coat hangers can be chosen to match the rest of your furnishing scheme. Paint wooden hangers in paint left over from other decorating projects, or buy sample-size tester pots to acquire the right colors in small quantities—you'll need hardly any paint to cover half a dozen hangers. Or pad them with lightweight foam batting and make fabric covers to match cushions and drapes, finishing them with a ribbon bow or fragment of lace.

20 Simple drapes ▶

Bedroom drapes need to provide privacy, but you don't necessarily want to block out all light. Bed linen is perfect for making drapes as it comes in extra-wide measures, letting you create complete window drops from a single width. Sew simple drapes from white linen sheeting, turning the tops over in a deep fold to make instant valances and trimming the edges with neat braid or decorative bobbles. For the most professional finish, look for sheets embroidered with a monogram or some other design to form an ornamental centerpiece for the valance.

Floating, gauzy fabrics are ideal for bedrooms as they screen the glass without totally blocking the light.

COUNTRY IDEAS FOR BEDROOM WINDOWS

● *Embroidered screens* Small windows can be neatly covered by a simple shade converted from a decorative cotton traycloth or linen antimacassar. Turn one of the narrow ends to make a channel about 1inch (2.5cm) deep, and thread it onto a curtain wire or slim rod. These shades are perfect for narrow casement windows, where you can fix the wire or rod onto the top of the frame itself, so the shade opens with the window.

● *Sheer curtains* The elegant alternative to old-fashioned nets, voile, cheesecloth, silk, and organza have a floating, gauzy quality that fills bedrooms with romance. Embroidered patterns, appliquéd beads, or mother-of-pearl buttons will add individual design details.

● *Ribbon edging* Small cottagey windows need small-scale prints and neat curtain treatments. To avoid swamping the space with pattern, use panels of plain white or colored cotton and trim the edges with contrasting braid or ribbon. Add a row of matching ribbon ties along the top, or tie decorative bows onto the rings. ◀

● *Skylight curtains* Attic rooms with sloping ceilings can present a problem, as windows fitted at an angle need special treatment. The simplest solution is to slot lightweight curtains onto wires at both top and bottom of the window, and use ribbon or cord to tie the gathered fabric out of the way during daylight hours.

● *Dormer rods* Dormer windows built out from the roof can take normal curtains, but the fabric needs to be rationed so that it doesn't obscure the limited glazed area. Instead of gathering the drapes to one side, fit them on hinged rods that will swing back from the window, lying flat along the sides of the dormer recess and leaving the glass clear.

● *Lace panels* Pick delicately woven figuring that will create a filigree pattern against the window as the light shines through it. Keep the panel flat rather than gathering it, so the pattern isn't disturbed and the effect doesn't become too frilly.

Gingham ribbon makes a cheerful trim along the edge of this plain muslin curtain—perfect for a small bedroom window.

TRADITIONAL BEDROOM STORAGE IDEAS

● *Hatboxes* Perfect for holding smaller items such as gloves, scarves, and belts—as well as the hats they were designed to take—these will stand neatly on shelves or on top of a closet, or can be stacked, several together, in a corner.

● *Curtained shelving* Open shelving establishes a friendly, accessible feel in a bedroom, much as it does in the kitchen, and is a useful alternative to bulky chests and closets in smaller rooms or where narrow staircases make access tricky for large furniture. Keep shelves dust-free by screening them with fabric panels gathered into neat curtains or fitted with a simple pull-up shade mechanism.

● *Suitcases* Look for old leather trunks and cases that can be stacked stagecoach-style, in descending order of size, to hold spare bed linen, towels, and clothes that you want to pack away for a season.

● *Linen chests* Wooden blanket boxes and big lidded laundry baskets will stand at the end of the bed to hold extra covers and spare duvets and pillows, and provide a useful tabletop at the same time. Use one next to the bed as an alternative side table—with enough room to take a lamp, clock, pile of night reading, and clutch of photographs—or position it under a window, topped with cushions to provide a comfortable windowseat.

● *Peg-rails* These are particularly useful in children's rooms and nurseries, helping you keep the floor clear and letting you hang coats, hats, and scarves, as well as drawstring bags to hold toys, laundry, and crush-resistant clothing.

● *Craftsman's miniatures* These elegant little chests of drawers, usually made as exhibition pieces to demonstrate the maker's ability or as prototypes of full-size furniture designs, are perfect for hiding away jewelry, makeup, pill bottles, and so on. Enjoy the grain of the original wood, or look for modern versions in medium-density fiberboard or inexpensive pine, and paint or decoupage them to your own design.

● *Shoeboxes* An incredibly useful size for filing letters and photographs, these make pretty bedroom storage if covered with fabric or decorative paper. Also look out for attractively covered box files: they are just as handy in the bedroom as on study shelves. ◀

Functional boxes can be covered in decorative paper or fabric to provide neat bedroom storage for letters, photographs, and small accessories.

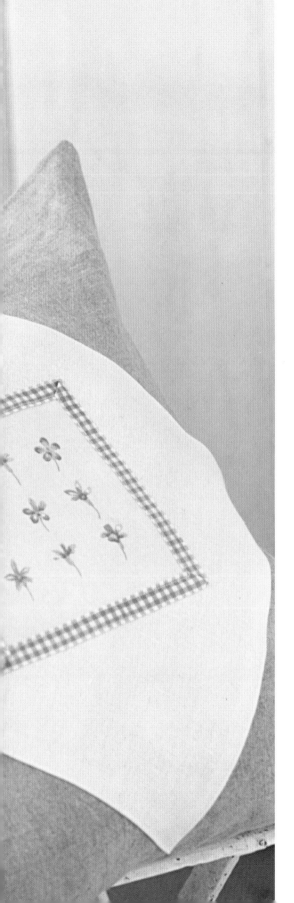

21 Bolsters and pillows ◄

For a sense of true indulgence, mix pillows and cushions in different sizes and pile them luxuriously on the bed. Long bolsters, standard rectangular pillows, big square designs reminiscent of old-fashioned French farmhouses, and little decorative hassock-style cushions can be distributed to bedroom chairs at night, then layered together on the bed during the day to make it a place to read and relax.

22 Hand-trimmed bed linen

Customize your bed linen to create individual designs with classic country style by trimming duvets and pillowcases with antique fabrics and remnants from other decorating projects. Edge white linen pillowcases with lengths of old lace and eyelet embroidery, patch patterned shapes onto plain cotton duvet covers, and cover functional buttons with fabric scraps so they create colorful details against the background fabrics.

23 Herbs and pomanders

Scented pomanders and other traditional bedroom fragrances will perfume your closets and linens and help protect fabrics from moths. Stitch handfuls of dried lavender flowers into little bags and sachets to bury among your clothes, and weave them into beribboned wands. Bunch a handful of flower-clustered stalks together and tie them just below the heads with a 2-yard (2-m) length of purple ribbon. Then bend back the stems so they enclose the flowers and weave the remaining ribbon in and out of the stems until the heads are completely covered, tying the loose ends in a neat bow.

24 Decorative sachets

Traditional bedroom linens provide some of the prettiest possible ready-made fabric panels for you to turn into practical accessories. Look out for them in second-hand shops and collectors' markets as well as recycling any spares of your own. Pillowcases are the perfect size to make laundry bags if you gather the opening into a drawstring neck, while delicate dressing table runners, decorated with lace, cutwork, or embroidery, can be folded and stitched into little buttoned sachets to hold handkerchiefs, jewelry, or toiletries.

Collect pillows and cushions in different shapes and sizes to add a luxurious finish to beds and chairs.

25 Wallpaper images

Use panels of wallpaper to line the backs of shelves and closets and the bases of drawers inside chests and dressing tables, cutting pieces to fit instead of using ready-made drawer liners. Ornate patterns that might be too overpowering if used over a larger area will add color and interest in small quantities, confined by the woodwork frame of a closet or the walls of a recess. Cut smaller pieces to frame as pictures, choosing a particular motif such as a flower or bird as a figurative image, or simply mounting an abstract pattern inside a neat frame.

26 Homemade rose water

For the instant fragrance of fresh roses, spray your bed linen with scented water before pressing it. Add a generous handful of fresh rose petals to a large pan of water. Bring it to a boil, simmer for one minute, then remove the pan from the heat and leave it for 12 hours so the scent infuses the water. Strain and decant the rose water into a sterile bottle with a tightly fitting lid, then transfer it to a spray container and spray onto your linens just before ironing them.

27 Pretty ceramics ▶

Collect pretty ceramics to hold jewelry, makeup, absorbent cotton, and other dressing table essentials. Junk stores and flea markets will provide good hunting grounds. China that is slightly damaged, or too fragile for practical service in the sitting room or on the dining table, will be perfect for lighter bedroom use. Mix elegant designs in among decorative scent bottles, pill boxes, and colored glass to create a dainty display. Use little vases and glass tumblers to hold makeup brushes and lavender wands (see tip 23 on page 79 for instructions). Collect pieces in a particular theme or color for a coordinated look, perhaps to match the style of the bedroom, or enjoy the contrasts of a more random mix of items.

A collection of dainty ceramics and silver-topped glass makes a pretty display on a bedroom table and can also be used for holding jewelry and makeup accessories.

CHAPTER FIVE

Studies

Every home needs a space away from the bustle of life. The chances are that such a spot

will be taken over by children's schoolwork and domestic paperwork—but the best studies are

places of perfect retreat, where you can surround yourself with your favorite books, pictures,

and music. What you should be aiming to achieve is a combination of restful atmosphere and

practical storage space, the sort of room in which everything works so simply that each task

you undertake feels less onerous because of the setting. Color and texture will go a long way

to help create the right background; mellow painted and worn leather furniture will add

gentle practicality; household objects commandeered from other rooms provide ingenious

storage; and traditional desk accessories will keep the effect comfortably elegant

rather than frighteningly ordered.

COLOR AND STYLE

1 Faded fabrics and distressed surfaces ◄

Certain rooms benefit more than others from a sense of wear and past use, and the study is one of them. Anything that emphasizes the idea of industry, of projects labored over and work completed here, will add to the room's history and enrich its ability to inspire more creativity. Look out for faded fabrics and worn, battered furniture, enjoying the marks that tell its story.

2 Bloomsbury style

Painted furniture will confer an artistic, creative look on your study, faintly reminiscent of Bloomsbury style. It's a forgiving surface that acquires extra character with wear and use, and doesn't demand careful handling or perfect color-scheming with other furnishings. Mix different colors freely, combining plain wood with mellow paintwork and simple freehand or stenciled patterns. You can seal it with a coat of matte varnish if you want to protect it, but don't worry too much about a perfect finish, as the simplicity of this look is half its charm.

An old kitchen table can be transformed into a writing desk or painting table, with plenty of space to work. Pictures on the walls make this study homely.

3 Old leather

The comfortable look of old leather furniture is automatically associated with studies and libraries. Mellow and traditional, it glows with the colors of the hedgerow and adds a distinctive texture almost like wood. Look for well-worn chairs and don't worry about the odd ink stain or scuff mark. They are all part of the furniture's history, and help to keep the effect informal.

4 Homemade pictures ▶

Decorate the walls with the family's hand-painted pictures, homemade artefacts, and collected treasures to surround you with creativity and promote inspiration. The study is a good place to make a display of favorite finds from country walks, so devise neat ways of turning the classic nature table into a framed exhibit that will hang on a wall or stand on the mantelshelf. Old drawers from printers' cabinets, divided into tiny compartments once used for storing metal lettering blocks, are perfect for holding small items such as seed coats and dried leaves.

Homemade pictures crafted from dried leaves in painted frames are a chance to display country treasures as well as decorating the room.

COUNTRY COLORS TO INSPIRE YOUR WORK

● *Leaf green* The color of nature and regeneration, green has a sobering, meditative quality that promotes industry and refreshes the spirit. Keep the shades soft and pale or deep and muted—nothing too bright and acidic.

● *Russet red* Touches of red are helpful for action, energy, and decision-making. Use crisp, clear fruit and berry shades for the most vibrant effect, or opt for rich autumnal coppers and terra-cottas for a more mellow, hedgerow feel.

● *Earth naturals* Neutral colors are calming and grounding, their plain, practical character suiting the work ethic of a traditional study. Enjoy mixing different wood shades and grains, and let shadows and textures add their own unique pattern.

● *Soft lilac* Shades of soft and restful purple have a clear, tranquil quality that is unbeatable for creativity and inspiration, and particularly good if you see your study as a personal retreat as well as a workroom.

● *Sunshine yellow* Glowing and light-reflective, yellows are particularly good for rooms that enjoy morning light, where their natural vitality recharges the energy of the space and creates a stimulating, invigorating working environment.

IDEAS TO BORROW FROM THE SCHOOLROOM

● *Old furniture* There's something touchingly nostalgic about those ink-stained desks—complete with their own drop-in inkwells—that still bear the scratches and scribblings of semesters past. If you want a computer desk you'll need a flat tabletop, but otherwise you could opt for the sort with a sloping surface that lifts up to store books and papers underneath.

● *School clocks* The huge, imposing designs that counted the minutes so slowly in class have a distinctive style that's perfect for a study wall.

● *Globes* Always useful for quick-reference location checking, this is also a classic design that will sit comfortably on any study desk or mantelshelf, and has far more charm than a computer route-finder program.

● *Reference books* Every study should have a basic library including an atlas, dictionary, plant finder, and bird identification book—plus walking maps, guide books, and background reference for any other subject of special family interest. The more used the better, so look for well-thumbed copies in secondhand shops and flea markets.

● *Science equipment* From the simplest wooden counting frames to old geometry sets in velvet-lined wooden cases, old school paraphernalia designed with real attention to detail has a timeless appeal.

● *Wood-cased metronomes* Even if you haven't room for a piano in your study, these distinctive pyramid-shaped gadgets, designed to keep a musician's beat, make beautiful desktop accessories.

5 **Book-lined shelves**
Secondhand hardback books are often found for sale so cheaply in junk stores that you can virtually buy them by the yard to stock your shelves. Look for distinctive colors or jacket designs, and quirky titles that will entertain you while you work. For tight spaces where there isn't room for full-depth shelves, you can create a trompe l'oeil effect by cutting the books through just behind the spines and gluing these onto shallow shelves to give the impression of a fully lined bookcase.

6 **Three-dimensional display boxes**
You can create your own display frame for small objects by sticking empty matchboxes together. Lay the boxes out to create the size you want, including a few double-size boxes to vary the arrangement, then use double-sided tape to stick them all together. Neaten the outside edges with an extra layer of tape or paper, back the frame with an additional sheet of paper to strengthen the structure, then paint the whole thing with a few coats of white latex paint so that it provides a blank background for your finds.

7 **Bookends and leather bindings** ◀
Let books provide their own furnishings, the multicolored spines, intriguing titles, and gold-tooled lettering creating an extra layer of interest against the walls. If you run out of space for shelves and bookcases, add old-style bookends to hold a few more volumes on mantelshelves and windowsills. Stone corbels and weathered building bricks can be used in pairs to perform this service, or you can design your own bookends by filling plain glass tanks with marbles or pebbles, or weighting square tin tea caddies with sand or gravel.

Old leather-bound books add library style and a sense of tradition to even the most functional study space.

STORAGE AND SHELVING

8 **Wall-hung storage** ▶

In a country-style study, storage can become part of your furnishings, with attractive containers contributing color, pattern, and good design to the overall scheme. Make the most of the available wall space by hanging practical fabric wall pockets and elegant wirework baskets to hold stationery, equipment, and paperwork, and fix traditional flat-sided planters or flower containers to make wall-mounted pen holders.

9 **Traditional bookcases**

Make the most of small rooms by coaxing usable space out of forgotten corners. Look for spare wall surfaces above windows and doors where a couple of shelves could usefully be fitted. Build floor-to-ceiling shelves into recesses and alcoves, and consider colonizing the corridor or landing immediately outside the room as space for extra storage. Mix fixed shelves with freestanding bookcases to keep the effect comfortable and informal, and look out for tall cases—designed rather like grandfather clocks—that will stand neatly behind a door or against a pillar.

Wall-hung pockets can be used to store desk essentials and stationery neatly out of the way. Hang them on wooden peg-rails or decorative metal hooks.

10 **Desk essentials ▶**
Line up bright kitchen containers on your desktop to hold pens and other essentials. Pottery mugs are perfect for writing materials (and offer a new lease on life for favorite mugs suffering broken handles). Small pitchers will store scissors and craft knives with their blades safely out of the way. And tall earthenware pitchers and wine coolers will provide useful storage for things like rulers and long-handled paintbrushes that are often too long to fit in a standard desk drawer. For a more rustic look, include terra-cotta flower pots among the more colorful glazed ceramics, and for a traditional effect, use silver jugs and pewter tankards as impromptu penholders.

Pitchers and tankards will hold writing and painting equipment on a study desktop. Look for them in junk stores or flea markets.

11 **Artisan shelves**
Maintain a simple, artisan feel in your study by building rustic-style shelving from recycled fruit crates. Pile up a stack of scrubbed wooden crates, using different sizes to take different heights of books and files. Lay them on their sides and weight them carefully by loading each layer with a few of your heaviest books to keep the whole structure stable. Build them up slowly and, if you wish, paint them to match the room's color scheme.

Right: A traditional wicker basket co-opted to hold files and paperwork helps to take the high-tech edge off a home computer room.

COUNTRY-STYLE FILING SOLUTIONS

● **Toast racks** Just as useful on a writing desk as on the breakfast table, toast racks make very handy paper racks to file letters and postcards, or hold a neat supply of fresh envelopes in different sizes.

● **Patterned files** Look for decorative files, covered in pretty fabric or paper, that can stand alongside your books on a shelf to file domestic papers, bills, and so on.

● **Covered shoeboxes** Just the right size to hold letters, postcards, photographs and appointment cards, these can be painted or covered with paper or fabric and will stack in a neat pile on a desk or shelf. Attach a metal frame to one end of each box so that you can slot in a card identifying the contents.

● **Flatware trays** Neatly designed wooden or basketweave trays are perfect for writing tables, their individual compartments providing slots for pens, pencils, erasers, scissors, pencil sharpeners, and other desk essentials.

● **Scallop shells** Use large flat-bottomed shells to keep stationery tidy on your desktop; they're just the right size for holding things like thumbtacks and paper clips.

● **Basket trays** Shallow rectangular woven baskets make perfect document trays and provide a softer alternative to filing cabinets. Think of the basket drawers fitted in some kitchen designs as a rough guide to size, and tie on plain brown luggage tags to label the contents. ▶

12 Baskets and bins ▼

Baskets and bins make excellent storage. Use them to hold bolts of fabric, rolls of drawing paper and giftwrap, and anything that is too long to fit in a drawer or too fragile to leave lying flat. All you need to do is weight the base with a few large pebbles so the whole thing won't overbalance if it becomes top-heavy.

13 Peg-rails and Shaker boxes

The Shakers were masters of practical design, and classic Shaker style has the neat, functional look that even country-style studies really need. Fix wooden peg-rails to the walls to hold bags of sewing scraps and craft equipment, and use the traditional rounded cherrywood boxes in different sizes to hold everything from thread spools and paints to stationery and business cards.

14 Small-scale storage ▶

The smaller and neater you can keep your storage furniture, the better organized your study will be. It doesn't need to be specifically designed for office or desktop use, so make the most of kitchen spice cabinets and craftsmen's miniature chests, fitted with tiny drawers that are perfect for holding beads, buttons, pens, and paper clips, as well as personal documents such as passports and birth certificates. Or cover a number of different-sized lidded boxes in matching paper. The important thing is to know exactly where everything is, and these neat storage systems will make life easier.

Left: Use open baskets to hold rolls of paper and bolts of fabric that you don't want to store folded.
Right: Pretty boxes in different sizes make neat storage for letters, writing materials, pens, and craft equipment.

DESKS AND SEATING

15 **Adaptable furniture** ◄
If you have no option but to carve your study out of another room, look for pretty furniture that will blend with the existing furnishings. Adaptable seating will make a big difference. A painted dining chair could be borrowed for occasional use at your writing desk (although it shouldn't be relied on for lengthy work sessions, when you'll need something with good back support) while a fabric-slung director's chair, chosen to match the color of your desk, can be turned to face into the room when needed for extra seating in a living space.

16 **Traditional writing desks**
Office desks can look grim and imposing, not the most inviting of settings to inspire you to creative work or lessen the chore of tackling household finances. For softer effects, look for traditionally styled bureaux and escritoires, painted in elegant country shades, and fitted with pigeonholes and secret drawers to hold stationery and paperwork. Neatest of all are those designed with a front that can be folded down into a desktop or closed to present a pretty façade to the room.

Comfortable sitting room furniture will adapt easily if you want to use a corner of the room as a study or home office.

COUNTRY-STYLE DESK LAMPS

● *Hand-painted shades* Give rein to your creativity and design your own hand-painted effects, keeping the patterns relaxed and freehand for a suitably simple Bloomsbury look. Use a plain white paper or cotton lampshade as your base, then mix poster or fabric paints to the colors you want. Combine areas of solid color with flowing, "script-like" strokes, leaving the shade unpainted where you want white highlights.

● *Button trims* Plain plastic buttons have a neat, practical quality that makes them perfect for workplaces, especially if you are planning to use yours as a sewing room. Collect different shapes and colors and use them to create a border around the rim, or to create patterns following the line of the shade.

● *Candle lamps* Scribbling by candlelight conjures up the classic romance of the writer's retreat, but is neither comfortable nor safe for anything more than the occasional flight of fancy. Authentic-looking candlestick bases, however, will provide an attractive alternative that looks like the real thing with none of the practical drawbacks.

● *Practical angles* Traditional office desk lamps, designed with a jointed base so the head can be angled to focus the beam where you need it, have a classic simplicity of style and function that makes them suitable for country studies as well as more industrial settings. Look for genuine office lamps with a used, worn appeal, or take advantage of modern replicas now available in pretty colors to match a soft, domestic color scheme.

● *Woven willow* Cut lengths of slim willow branches and use them to cover a plain upright lampbase, binding them with garden twine at intervals and at the top and bottom to keep them

in place. Fit the base with a natural-style shade in plain parchment or decorated with leaves to continue the hedgerow theme.

● *Classic plumes* Take inspiration from the quill pens of the traditional writer's study, and decorate a plain shade with elegant feathers. The delicate plumage provides natural patterning rather like wood grain, and the tips of the feathers give the rim of the shade a natural scalloped trim. ▲

A shade trimmed with elegant feathers will turn an everyday lamp into a country-style desk light.

17 Kitchen tables
In the absence of a proper bureau or writing desk, an old kitchen table in plain scrubbed pine will supply your study with a practical work surface which is especially helpful if you want to tackle sewing or craft projects and can make good use of the larger tabletop. Make sure the height is comfortable for you to work at and, if possible, try to find a table fitted with a cutlery drawer underneath, to hold pens, brushes, stationery, and so on. (You may occasionally come across designs with drawers at both ends, or a single deep drawer that can be opened from both sides of the table).

18 Foldaway desktops
Where there isn't room for a full-time office, a drop-leaf table makes an excellent temporary desk in a sitting, dining, or bedroom. Folded back flat against the wall when not needed for work, it takes up barely any space, and can also be pressed into service as a side table to hold a lamp, telephone, or vase of flowers. When you need a writing desk, you simply pull up the folded leaf and instantly double the size of the tabletop.

19 Color scheming swatch boards ◄
If the study is to be the nerve center of your decorating and furnishing plans, you need plenty of space to map out your ideas and gauge the effect of different colors and patterns. Make a swatch board from a large piece of cork board, painted white or with plain white calico stretched over it to create a neutral background, and use it to try out samples of fabric and wallpaper. Pin your swatches to the board with thumbtacks, and add potential paint shades by painting patches of color onto white cardboard and pinning these in place too. Collect trimmings and accessories and add these to the planned scheme before making your final choices.

Create a practical swatch board on which you can try out wallpaper, fabric, and paint samples to develop your furnishing plans.

DETAILS AND ACCESSORIES

20 Garden buckets

Even the most functional details can convey a sense of country style, so don't let your study succumb to the dreary practicalities of a nine-to-five office. Raid the garden shed for galvanized buckets and wicker baskets to use as trash cans, or take an elegant wirework basket and line it with pretty fabric to make it practical for catching pencil shavings and used ballpoint pens, as well as wastepaper.

21 Covered notebooks ▷

Choose notebooks and files that suit the style of the room and add color, texture, or a touch of pattern to your study furnishings. Plain brown paper trimmed with string or raffia will reinforce the practical edge while maintaining a simple, natural look that prevents the setting from feeling too bleak and officelike. For a softer approach, look for stationery bound in pretty florals or simple checks, and save remnants of fabric and giftwrap to decorate plain covers.

Stock up on notebooks and files that suit the room's decor and inspire you to keep your work and papers in good order.

THINGS TO FRAME ON A STUDY WALL

● *Spelling charts* Simple school posters reminding you that "A is for apple" and "B is for boat" have a natural graphic style as well as nostalgic childhood charm.

● *Maps* Old illustrated maps showing state boundaries and historic landmarks are often small enough to frame. Larger-scale maps and maritime charts don't need framing but in effect provide their own wallpaper, decorating the room with interesting reference material.

● *Handwriting samples* Make a display of those classic templates once used to teach children elegant copperplate or neat script, with sequences of joined-up letters and painstakingly formed words.

● *Award certificates* Evidence of achievements and qualifications isn't something you can easily put on show, but the study is one room where it won't feel out of place. In particular, make a display of children's certificates for music exams, swimming, cycling, and other achievements.

● *Postage stamps* Franked envelopes have their own interest, evoking the time and place of their posting, but even unused stamps will create a graphic effect against a study wall. Frame a sheet of simple brightly colored stamps, or make a feature of special-issue celebration designs.

● *Letters and postcards* Again, it's the personal touch and handwritten script that provides the real interest. A short, beautifully composed letter thanking you for a present or invitation, or announcing some piece of significant news, is worth framing to evoke memories of the writer, or the event, whenever you read it. ▶

Neatly framed handwritten letters make intriguing decoration for a study wall.

22 Leather-trimmed blotters

Classic desks are often inset with a panel of leather to provide a cushioned writing surface and prevent indentations of pen marks on wood. If the leather is damaged, or you want to improvise a similar effect on a plain wooden desktop, add an old-fashioned leather-bound blotter with thick sheets of blotting paper slotted into leather corners.

23 Portable writing desks

Several centuries before high-tech designers came up with the idea of the laptop computer for people on the move, it was common for travelers to carry their writing materials with them in a portable writing desk—a wooden locking case designed to hold pens, ink, and paper inside, and with a sloping top providing you with a desk wherever you found yourself. These make an elegant addition to contemporary studies, where they still provide useful storage even if their portability is no longer strictly necessary.

24 Calligraphy and colored inks

For traditional desktop style, look for little wooden writing boxes that provide neat storage compartments for ink bottles and pens. Keep your desk stocked with inks in different colors—blue and black for official letters; purple, turquoise, and sepia for writing diary entries and notes to friends; gold and silver for decorative letterwork. Learn the art of classic calligraphy and add a few italic nibs in varying sizes to your collection so you can script elegant place cards, gift tags, and invitations.

A traditional bureau provides little drawers and pigeonholes for books, pens, stamps, and stationery, creating an elegant centerpiece for an old-fashioned study or writing room.

WHERE TO FIND SPACE FOR A COUNTRY STUDY

● *In a corner of the sitting room* A writing table and chair needn't take up much room or feel too obtrusive if you choose slim-line furniture designs and fit them into an existing corner or recess. A decorative screen will provide a very useful divide if you want to keep this area separate from the rest of the room.

● *In a closet* Even if you haven't a full-size walk-in closet to convert, it's worth looking out for clever furniture designs that will house a complete work system in a single elegant cabinet, so your computer, document files, and stationery can all be hidden neatly away behind closed doors and, when shut, the closet will look more like a traditional linen press than a fully functioning office.

● *On a landing* If the study will only be used occasionally, look for spare space outside bedrooms, where a narrow table won't take up much room and where it can be used for flowers or a display of photographs when not being used for writing.

● *In a guest bedroom* Being able to keep a room permanently available for guests is a luxury not all houses can afford. You may find that it's a better solution to turn a spare bedroom into a workspace for writing, sewing, craft projects, and dealing with domestic papers, but furnish it with a comfortable sofabed that can transform the room into a sleeping space for overnight guests when needed.

● *Under the stairs* Make use of "dead" space that wasted because it is too cramped or awkward for regular use. The low ceiling height will not be a problem because you will be sitting rather than standing, and the difficult triangle at the lower end of the stairs can be neatly used to stack filing baskets and crates—increasing from a single layer to three or four, to fill up the space like a jigsaw puzzle. ▶

25 Traditional letterheads

Decorate your letters with traditional embossed letterheads instead of using printed paper. Original embossing tools—designed like a classic hole-puncher but often beautifully ornamental, and with a relief surface that presses down to "stamp" your name or address into the paper—can be updated with your own details to let you emboss individual sheets of writing paper as you use them.

26 Stamps and sealing wax

Keep a supply of colored sealing wax and a personal initial or monogram seal so that you can give correspondence your own stamp and ensure its secrecy. Drip a small pool of wax onto the flap of the envelope, then press your seal carefully into it, and use it to personalize presents by adding your mark to parcels wrapped up in traditional brown paper and string.

27 Unusual paperweights

Look for intriguing objects to make desktop paperweights for keeping your documents in order. Borrow weights from a set of traditional kitchen scales. Scour secondhand shops for decorative trivets and flatirons—so often employed as doorstops, but just as useful as paperweights. Save pieces of architectural stone or plaster from building projects, and pick up pretty colored pebbles and other natural finds.

28 Bakelite telephones ▶

A classic Bakelite telephone will give your study a definite air of style and tradition. Black is the most familiar finish; you may also find designs in glossy red or luxurious cream, that will give your country study a slightly Art Deco feel. Make sure any phone you buy has been approved for connection and use, otherwise you will have to keep it for show only, enjoying its stately curves but not that distinctive old-fashioned ringing tone.

29 Decorative bulletin boards

Equip your study with a bulletin board and *aide-mémoire* by covering a large panel of cork or fiberboard with attractive paper or fabric so that messages and invitations can be pinned onto it with thumbtacks. For a more decorative effect, create a latticework of ribbon lengths crisscrossed over the board, letting you slip postcards and photographs under the ribbon without defacing them.

30 Elegant pens

For a romantic flourish, seek out distinctive pens that revive the traditional pleasure of letter writing. Classic marbled fountain pens, their delicate veined patterns gleaming with a faint iridescence, have a formal beauty to grace desktops and pen trays, while contemporary Venetian glass designs, swirling with twists of jewel-bright color, are gloriously decorative.

A small-scale wooden writing desk fitted into a snug recess beneath the stairs makes a neat study space for occasional use.

Give your study desk a retro feel with classic accessories such as an anglepoise lamp and Bakelite telephone.

CHAPTER SIX

Hallways and Landings

These forgotten spaces tend to be decorated as an afterthought and not treated with the same

care we afford individual rooms, but the contribution they make to the overall look and feel of the

house is immeasurable. The hall gives the first impression to guests and incomers, while landings

link other rooms, providing viewpoints and sightlines between them to define the character of the

larger space. These key areas can acquire country style in their own right. Neat furniture will help

you make the most of restricted spaces and highlight the architectural interest of awkward angles.

Inspiring colors will invite you in, open up the house, and provide an intriguing glimpse of the

rooms beyond. Simple accessories such as flowers, pictures, and books will create an instant

welcome that establishes your personal style right from the start.

COLORS AND FURNISHINGS

1 Welcoming colors ◄

One of the distinctive characteristics of country style is the sense of welcome that invites visitors into the house and creates enticing views from one room into another. Clever use of color can enhance this effect, with strong hues in distant rooms drawing the eye onward and establishing areas of interest to encourage exploration. Think of the house as one unified space, rather than a collection of separate rooms. Leave doors open to create intriguing sightlines, and leave lamps on in unoccupied rooms to highlight these views.

2 Console tables ►

Even the smallest hallway needs somewhere to collect mail and leave keys. This is where a slim table such as the classic console design comes in handy, standing neatly against the wall to provide a surface that's almost more a shelf than table. Some consoles are fashioned in a half-moon shape so they obstruct the space as little as possible, and stand on just three legs, with the back of the table fixed to the wall for support. A quirky alternative, if you have slightly more room, is a traditional sewing table, with the sewing machine itself folded down into the tabletop and the ironwork of the original wheel and treadle beneath providing an interesting feature against a plain wall.

A warm coral color is soft and welcoming in this Mediterranean-style rough-plastered hallway.

3 Potting benches

Given that most front doors lead in straight from the yard, it is perfectly natural to furnish your hall as a garden room, linking indoor and outdoor areas. Decorate the walls with botanical prints and use a simple wooden potting bench as a side table. Traditional potting benches provide at least two tiers, so you can use it to hold the usual hall accoutrements of lamp, telephone, and visitors' book, as well as stacking it with rustic accessories such as watering cans, old enamel buckets, and terra-cotta flowerpots. You might also find the lower level makes a practical storage rack for things like rubber boots and gardening shoes.

A traditional console table will stand flat against the wall, providing just enough space to hold various hall essentials.

QUICK WAYS TO CREATE
A WARM WELCOME

● *Seating* Providing your hall with somewhere to sit turns it into a room in its own right and establishes a real welcome from the outset. An armchair or small sofa—perfect for enjoying comfortable phone calls—makes the space feel relaxed and inviting.

● *Pictures* Provide immediate areas of interest by using hall walls for paintings and photographs. This will stamp your identity on your home and establish a sense of personal space.

● *Clocks* A ticking clock is like the heartbeat of a home, its gentle sound providing a reassuring presence in the background. For the warmest welcome, you really need a long-case grandfather clock, but big wall-mounted school or station clocks have their own character.

● *Fruit bowls* Fruits are as colorful as flowers and create homely arrangements, especially if you can display produce grown in your own yard and greenhouse.

● *Books* Always intriguing and characterful, books are an essential addition if you have room for them. Slot a collection between bookends on a windowsill or side table, or stand a slim bookcase against a free wall.

● *Flowers* Color and scent are key elements in bringing spaces to life, by arousing the senses and creating lively focal points. Go for simple displays of garden blooms rather than a formal arrangement. ▶

Fresh flowers and homely furniture will make the hall feel lived in, and more than just a passageway.

4 Natural floor coverings

Flooring materials such as coir and sisal have the neutral color of wood, and a tough, practical quality that matches the functional nature of spaces such as staircases and hallways. Be careful, when choosing flooring for stairs, to go for an option that will maintain its rough surface even after constant wear. Some materials tend to become smooth and shiny (which will compromise safety) or may sag and stretch out of shape. To keep the effect simple and traditional on stairs and landings, think about laying flooring in strips, or "runners," rather than having it fitted. Runners can be bound with plain or colored edging to give a neat finish.

5 Benches and settles ▼

Narrow benches—either simple plank–topped stands or wooden seats with high backs, in the style of a church pew—are perfect for halls and landings as they can do double duty as seating and tabletops. Stand them flat against the wall, adding cushions if you want to make them more comfortable.

A high-backed settle with plenty of cushions provides a comfortable place to sit without taking up too much room.

COLORS TO MAKE A COUNTRY IMPRESSION

● *Cobalt blue* A flash of bright color that will bring the house to life as soon as you open the door. A wonderful background for pictures, it combines beautifully with terra-cotta floor tiles for a Mediterranean contrast.

● *Primrose yellow* Soft and cottagey, this has the natural warmth of all yellows but is pale enough to be almost cream, with a delicate quality that catches the light and opens up small country hallways.

● *Emerald green* The natural color of fields and foliage heightened to a jewel-bright intensity, bringing the glory of the garden into the house. Add polished wood and leather for a stunning contrast.

● *Terra-cotta* Rich and glowing, the color of baked clay combines a natural earthy quality with the heat of spice shades. Use it to create instant drama and a generous welcome.

● *Antique white* The traditional background to country furnishings, this gentle white is mellow and forgiving, concealing rather than highlighting uneven wall surfaces and blending comfortably with natural materials such as stone and slate.

● *Soft putty* Quieter than terra-cotta but with much of its warmth; deeper and richer than creams and whites, this is a wonderfully versatile neutral. In some lights it can appear to have a subtle pinkish, chocolate, or coffee tinge, but it always stays restful and unobtrusive as a background shade.

6 Flagstone floors

Stepping onto a worn floor of old stone or brick is an instant indication that you have come home to a country house. If you want to recreate that look, reclaimed bricks and stone flags can be found at salvage centers. Alternatively, terra-cotta and quarry tiles will have much the same effect.

7 Simple staircases ◄

Leaving the stairs in their natural wood will provide a simple, mellow look, or, to lighten the gloom of a dark staircase, you can paint them white or a soft, neutral gray or cream. One option is to paint just the outer edges of the treads and risers, leaving the central area in plain wood, or to paint the central area in a color that matches the walls or other furnishings, creating the effect of a carpet runner against the contrasting white or cream of the outer edges.

8 Traditional stair rods

If you fit a runner or carpet, the classic way to finish it is with traditional stair rods —slim metal bars that sit in the "crook" of each stair, fixed tightly in place on either side so the carpet is stretched flat beneath them. Choose a metal that echoes the style of the house, avoiding the brightest brass, which tends to look smart and urban rather than mellow and country-style.

Left: Plain painted stair treads look neat and practical.
Right: An ornamental mirror will add decoration as well as increase the sense of light.

9 **Decorative mirrors** ◄
Mirrors always increase the sense of space and light, and this is especially useful in hallways—where both commodities may be in short supply—to create a welcoming first impression. Hang one large mirror, choosing an elegant frame that adds its own decoration, or arrange smaller ones in clusters, as though they were paintings.

PRACTICAL DETAILS

10 **Old-fashioned boot racks**
Ranks of rubber boots, in graduating sizes and different colors, are a fixture in country hallways. Instantly evocative of muddy fields and flooded lanes, they bring home their own supply of mud and create puddles on hall floors. Provide some sort of tray to let them drain, and a rack to keep them off the ground to avoid the worst of the footprints. Traditional boot racks will store boots upside down on wooden posts.

11 **Brushes and bootscrapers**
A tough square of traditional coconut matting will deal with the everyday onslaught of outdoor footwear on indoor floors, but you need to tackle the worst of the mud before it gets that far. An old-fashioned bootscraper fixed outside the front door will add a touch of classic practicality, designed with a metal bar on which you can remove debris from shoes and boots. A stiff brush or broomhead, wedged between a couple of large stones and upturned so that the bristles are on top, will help with dried mud.

QUICK IDEAS TO TRANSFORM A LANDING

● *Add a workspace* Add a small desk and chair and turn it into a writing area. Choose a position near a window to provide good working light and an inspiring view.

● *Linking colors* Paint landing doors and woodwork in interesting colors to forge links between rooms and continue themes from one to the next. Pick up colors visible through open doors and use them for door frames and picture rails so the shades play and bounce off one another.

● *Book shelves* Make use of spare space to add an extra bookcase or fit a set of shelves. The average paperback is only 4½ inches (110cm) wide, so the shelves can be very shallow and barely take up any space, while helping to furnish the landing as a room in its own right.

● *Extra seating* Paint a traditional-style wooden garden bench (lightweight, compact designs are available in assemble-it-yourself kits) add a few pillows, and set it on a landing as a focal point.

● *Picture gallery* Use a landing wall or alcove to display a set of pictures such as black-and-white family photos or architectural prints, so the defined space creates a frame for the collection.

● *A place to read* Provide a comfortable armchair, or a little sofa or chaise longue, and enjoy it as a place to read, away from the main rooms of the house and with different views and sightlines from the ones you normally see. ▶

A comfortable chair or sofa will turn a square landing into a little extra sitting room.

12 Baskets and trays

Most country halls become a jumble of shoes and boots, as footwear is changed for different activities, from horse riding, gardening, and fishing to gentler (and less grubby) indoor pursuits. It's worth lining up a row of baskets or wooden crates against one wall to keep these tidy and collect any strays until they can be claimed by their owners.

13 Elegant banisters

The design of your staircase has a huge impact on the rest of the hall. You may not be able to alter the angle, but you can change the banisters to create a different look. Slim wooden spindles can replace chunkier posts, and painting them in a light color may have a more elegant effect than plain wood. Iron banisters often look more graceful: these can be polished, or painted black, or a lighter color.

14 Coat pegs and coatracks

Fix old-fashioned peg-rails and coat hooks to hall walls, attaching them at different levels for adults and children. Where there is less room, use a coat stand that can hold a quantity of coats and hats in a neat space. Or, if you are concerned that casual country style might degenerate into chaos without careful supervision, install a large freestanding closet in which your family can hide outdoor clothes away to keep the hallway clear of clutter.

15 Traditional umbrella stands

Use traditional country containers to improvise deep-welled umbrella stands. Terra-cotta planters from the garden, including urns and troughs, are practical for this purpose as long as they haven't got drainage holes in the bottom.

16 Country-style doorstops ▶

All kinds of domestic items can be pressed into practical and decorative service around the house. Among the most useful are old-fashioned flatirons and shoe lasts. The irons, which used to be heated over a fire or kitchen range until they reached a suitable temperature for pressing fabrics, are heavy enough to make excellent doorstops, either resting upright or flat on the ground so the point can be wedged under the door if necessary. Or you can employ traditional lasts, their smooth wooden bases solid and sculptural, as an alternative.

17 Rope handrails

For a simple, artisan effect, you might consider fixing a rope handrail against one wall of your staircase instead of a conventional banister. Threaded through sturdy metal loops attached to the wall at intervals so that the rope hangs in gentle swags rather than being pulled taut, this gives the staircase a slightly nautical feel.

Look out for intriguing objects such as ironwork and statuary to make alternative doorstops.

DECORATIVE ACCESSORIES

18 **Beeswax and lavender** ▶
A bowl of well-chosen flowers will scent your home from the moment you enter, but other, more subtle fragrances can play their part in establishing a sense of authentic country life. The distinctive aroma of old furniture polished with beeswax, a hint of lavender escaping from closets and chests that hold clothes or linen, and the delicious mixes of homemade potpourri are all timeless country scents. For a classic potpourri, combine flowers such as lavender and rose petals with spices and a sprinkling of essential oils, refreshing it with a few more drops of oil now and then.

19 **Traditional visitors' books**
Add a visitors' book so your guests can leave their impressions of the house, and so you have a record of events and people you want to remember. Leather- or fabric-bound books will give your hall table a traditional look, or you can design your own homemade book by binding sheets of thick parchment or cartridge paper inside a decorative cover. Provide a good-quality pen, too, so your guests' writing appears at its best, and perhaps a set of colored crayons so children can add their own memories in picture form.

Informally displayed flowers and natural wood provide an instant welcome and reinforce the country style of the home.

20 Picture galleries ▶

Halls and staircases can be among the most interesting places to display paintings and photographs, as the wall space is defined by specific boundaries and—in the case of stairs—not cluttered up by furniture. Use a corridor to hang a gallery of pictures providing interest at eye level along its length, or accent the sweep and ascent of a staircase by positioning paintings so they follow its line.

WHAT TO DISPLAY ON WALLS AND SHELVES

● *Bells* Some old houses still have the original bells that were used to summon servants to specific rooms. Otherwise, panels can occasionally be picked up in flea markets or junk stores and fixed to the wall to add a touch of traditional character.

● *Gardening tools* The worn wooden handles and intriguing shapes of hoes, rakes, forks, and spades make dramatic silhouettes against a plain wall and provide a reminder of country life.

● *Watering cans* Their hooped handles and elongated spouts make a robust alternative to a display of china, even if the metal is rusted or damaged. Line them up along a shelf or bench—including one or two for practical use if possible.

● *Broomsticks and carpet beaters* Contrasting shapes of traditional cleaning items, from simple carpet beaters to the old-fashioned birch besom usually associated with witches, will conjure up a sense of domestic history and practical country style.

Left: A simple painted tongue-and-groove wall provides the perfect backdrop for a colorful country-style wreath, made with hedgerow finds gathered on a country walk.

Right: Contrasting game feathers wired into a plain base create an unusual wreath in neutral colors.

HOMEMADE WREATHS FOR YOUR DOOR

● ***Dried roses*** Use a metal coat hanger as your base, bending it into a circle or, for a touch of romance, into a heart shape. Weave lengths of freshly cut jasmine or clematis around the frame to cover the metal, then attach dried rose heads with fine florist's wire and hang the wreath by its hook.

● ***Hydrangeas*** Choosing three or four different varieties or colors for a subtle contrast, gather the heads into small bunches and tie them onto a florist's wire wreath with green raffia, creating a full, multipetaled effect.

● ***Gypsophila*** Start with a circle of floral foam. Soak it well, then pierce with short stems of white-blossomed gypsophila until it is thickly covered with foliage and flowers. To keep the wreath fresh, water the foam base every two days.

● ***Crab apples*** Unravel a wire coat hanger, bending it into a circle but leaving the ends unjoined. Thread crab apples onto the wire until it is completely covered with the bright fruit except for a couple of bare inches at either end. Overlap these ends and bind them with florist's wire to complete the circle.

● ***Blackberries and sloes*** Cut long stems of brambles and weave them together into a wreath with strands of sloes so the different-colored berries glow like hedgerow jewels.

● ***Woven willow*** Lengths of willow or other thin, pliable branches make solid bases for rustic wreaths. Buy them ready-made from a good garden supplier and leave them plain or decorate them with feathers, nuts, and autumnal seed coats.

● ***Birdseed*** Hang a wreath of grasses, grains, and seeds near your door to attract garden birds (but do make sure it's out of the reach of local cats). Starting with a thick-gauge wire circle, weave stems such as oats and wheat to cover it, then decorate with sunflowers and poppy seed coats.

● ***Feathers*** Pick strong, sleek feathers rather than soft fluffy ones. Make a circle of twisted wire as your base, then wire the feathers onto it one by one, overlapping them to conceal the fixings and to create a more luxurious effect.

DOORS AND WINDOWS

21 Simple door designs ◄

Traditional doors make all the difference to landings, where entrances and exits are an intrinsic part of the furnishings. Simple paneled doors, usually designed as two long panels above two short ones, with a crosspiece in between, are classically elegant, and the upper panels can be replaced with plain or decorative glass if you want to increase the light flow through the house. In more rustic style, basic "planked" doors are created from upright lengths of wood slotted together and secured with a couple of horizontal lengths, and sometimes a diagonal too. These are often fitted with old-fashioned latches rather than turning handles, supplying an extra touch of country style.

22 Knobs and knockers

Traditional ironwork lends a distinctive finish to front doors. Look for cast-iron doorknobs, knockers, and mailboxes. Forage in architectural salvage centers for original designs that can be recycled, and seek out new craftsman-made pieces fashioned along authentic lines. Decorative old keys have their own charm. They don't need to have any practical use—just collect interesting shapes and hang them from a row of hooks.

23 Elegant windows

Hall windows don't invariably need drapes. A glowing window providing a view of a beautiful interior is far more inviting from the outside than a blank panel of fabric. If the window itself is elegant, you might be better off leaving it unscreened and using the sill as a display shelf. Shapely fittings and handles will add their own decoration, the slim stays and intricate curls of traditional wrought-iron craftsmanship creating interesting patterns against the woodwork of the frame.

24 Stained-glass effects

Stained glass will add extra beauty to windows, casting colored reflections onto floors and walls as the sun streams through them during the day, and providing a view of glowing panels of color from the outside when the hall and stairs are illuminated at night. Occasional stained-glass panes in a plain window will have more subtlety than the full-blown church effect, and you can achieve something of the same look by standing colored glassware in the window where the light will catch it. Vases, bottles, and goblets can be displayed on the sill or on glass shelves fitted across the window.

Simple planked doors with traditional ironwork create an instant country effect and are a neat alternative for small, cottage-style rooms.

CLASSIC IDEAS FOR OUTDOOR STYLE

● *Fences and railings* Use local materials and traditional techniques to provide your house with picket fences, dry stone walls, willow hurdles, or elegant wrought-iron railings.

● *Pathways* Weathered brick can be laid in straight lines or herringbone patterns, old stone flags can be interspersed with patches of herbs, and paths of soft, springy chamomile will scent the air as you crush the leaves underfoot. Look for old terra-cotta rope edging, designed in a continuous coil effect, for a traditional finish.

● *Potted trees* Create a miniature avenue along the pathway with little trees of box, bay, and holly, or set a pair to stand sentinel on either side of your door.

● *Lanterns and Christmas tree lights* Light the pathway with candle lanterns at night, hang them in an arch over your gate, and trail tiny white Christmas tree lights along windowboxes and around potted trees.

● *Old-fashioned doorbells* The traditional design was worked by a pull-knob set into the wall beside the door, but even without the full working mechanism, a schoolroom-style cast-iron bell hung at the entrance creates a distinctive effect.

● *Benches* Create a welcome even before your guests get inside. Stand a solid wooden seat or an old-fashioned park bench beside the path or beneath a window. Or, if you have a porch over your door, build bench seats into it on either side, rather like a lych-gate. ▶

A wooden bench beside the front door extends your home's sense of welcome and provides a place to sit on sunny days.

CHAPTER SEVEN

Bathrooms

The true country bathroom is never cold or clinical. However simple its furnishings, it conveys a sense of homely warmth and comforting domesticity, where surfaces such as plain wood and bare metalwork are mellowed by soft fabrics, pretty china, graceful furniture, and the sweet fragrance of fresh-cut flowers. Freestanding bathtubs and washstands add a sense of timeless comfort far removed from the sleek, characterless luxury of smart modern fittings, while elegant little tables and chairs make it a room to spend time in rather than a purely functional space. The secret is to keep the background as understated as possible and use the accessories to add color, warmth, and decoration. Practical flooring, restrained pattern, and traditional styling will all play their part, and the subtle weaves of old-fashioned waffle towels and translucent voile window panels will add delicate detail.

COLOR AND PATTERN

1 Relaxing colors

Choose colors to help you relax as well as to conjure up a sense of the country. Blues, greens, and aquas will reflect the shades of the sea and evoke a tranquil, refreshing mood. Warmer creams, neutrals, and soft whites have the Zen-like calm of their natural quality, which can be enhanced by the inclusion of materials such as chalk, wood, and stone. Touches of sweeter, floral color, such as pinks, lilacs, and corals, will add restful details, helping to turn your bathroom into a true country retreat.

2 Pretty linens ▼

Bathroom linens supply the room with much of its comfort factor, so think of their colors and textures as part of your furnishings. Plain white for bath sheets, hand towels, and bath mats is still the classic option, but elegant patterns worked into the weave will add white-on-white luxury, and other colors and patterns can be incorporated in trimmings and edgings made from gingham ribbon or floral-printed cotton. Look for soft cotton waffle towels with pastel-colored jacquard edgings, and plain, crisp cotton panels trimmed with decorative lace.

3 Wood paneling ▶

Wood-paneled walls are softer and warmer than flat painted surfaces, helping to take the chilly edge off the cool white of classic porcelain fixtures. Ready-to-fit paneling is available in different designs, with square or rectangular panels creating a traditional, elegant look suitable for period-style rooms and tongue-and-groove planking adding a simpler finish. Both are perfect for covering up cracked or uneven plastering. You'll also find that if you fit tongue and groove horizontally in a narrow bathroom, it will have the effect of widening the space.

4 Country-style tiles

Bathrooms don't need to be tiled from top to bottom—in fact a vast expanse of tiles can make the room feel uncomfortably clinical—but choosing the right tiles will enhance rather than undermine a sense of country style. Plain ceramics can glow with Mediterranean color, any variations in shade and intensity highlighting their handmade character beneath the glaze. Traditional patterns such as blue-and-white Delft designs or more rustic images can be used to add occasional interest without dominating the room. And natural stone can be used on walls as well as floors for a mellow, farmhouse look.

Left: Colorful braid adds a neat edging to plain white cotton towels.

Right: Tongue-and-groove paneling helps to give this country bathroom a warmer feel, lining the walls and also creating a neat surround for the bathtub.

DISTINCTIVE LOOKS FOR COUNTRY BATHROOMS

● *Country-house elegance* Keep the look graceful and old-fashioned, with faded floral patterns on the walls, and remnants of fine dining-room china to hold soaps and toothbrushes.

● *Simple Shaker* Plain lines and wood paneling are perfect for understated country bathrooms, creating an air of calm laced with practical touches such as peg-rails and wall cabinets.

● *Classic romance* Install a deep rolltop bathtub and bathe in candlelit splendor. Indulge in opulent colors such as gold and purple, and swag the room with luxuriously draped fabric.

● *Old-fashioned utility* Recreate the homey, thrift-conscious style from the 1940s and 50s, when simple comforts were coaxed out of basic materials such as enamel, galvanized tin, and plain scrubbed wood. Look for enamel soap dishes and water pitchers, wooden towel racks, wood-handled brushes, and slatted duckboard floor panels.

● *Caribbean sunshine* Enjoy a splash of carnival sunshine with the vivid colors of the Caribbean. Paint woodwork in bright parrot blues and greens, with towels and accessories in cheerful reds and yellows. Shade the windows with slatted shutters and add painted, carved exotic birds and flying fish.

● *Planked beach-house* Fit painted tongue-and-groove paneling, reminiscent of American clapboard buildings and traditional beach houses, and furnish the room with bright cottons and seaside accessories. ▶

Beach-house paneling and seaside accessories combine well with bright cotton rugs and simple basket storage.

BATHROOM FABRICS TO CONJURE UP QUICK COUNTRY STYLE

● *Gingham* The classic fabric for simple country bathrooms, these neat cotton checks in their bright colors are just perfect for making lightweight curtains and drawstring laundry bags, or for trimming towels. Use blues and greens to match a cool watercolor scheme, or reds and yellows to add a warmer, more cheerful touch.

● *Cotton lace* Lace adds a delicate touch wherever you use it. In bathrooms, the designs to look for are the heavier, more loosely woven trims that edge traditional-style hand towels and washstand runners.

● *Rosebuds* Conjure up a traditional country look by using pretty sprigged cotton in gentle colors for curtains and wash bags, and to cover padded coat hangers.

● *Waffle* The dimpled, textured cotton used to make traditional towels has the warmth of the more usual fluffy terrycloth, but also a neat crispness that looks far more elegant when folded on a rail or draped over the side of the bathtub. Use it to create a fabric backing to a waterproof shower curtain, so the waterproof layer is concealed and the whole effect appears less functional.

● *Embroidery* For a subtly decorative finish that recognizes the value of fine details and skilled stitchcraft, look for white-on-white embroidered designs and personalize plain linens with elegant monograms. ▶

Monogrammed linens and ornate mirrors help to create a sense of old-fashioned luxury in a country bathroom.

TRADITIONAL IDEAS FOR BATHROOM FLOORS

● *Linoleum* Rehabilitated after years in the furnishing wilderness, the appeal of linoleum is its organic structure, a combination of natural ingredients including cork, linseed, and wood, all compressed onto a jute or burlap backing. Elegant checkered patterns in smart black and white or soft creams and aquas provide a classic background for traditional bathroom fittings.

● *Painted boards* Painting a wooden floor white or soft cream will lighten the whole room and make it feel more spacious, while maintaining a sense of pared-down style that combines simplicity with comfort. ◀

Painted floors and freestanding cabinets add a practical look slightly reminiscent of Shaker style.

● *Matting* Adding cotton rugs or rush matting will make the room feel more furnished and save you from indulging in a luxuriously fitted carpet.

● *Plain wood* Natural floorboards are mellow and warm underfoot and their understated neutrality will adapt to any color scheme. Waxes and varnishes can adjust the shade of the wood as well as sealing the finish; liming or bleaching will whiten it slightly, giving a paler, cooler tone.

● *Ceramic tiles* Mellow quarry, terra-cotta, and limestone will create a natural look that mixes well with plain white linens and pale wood accessories.

FURNITURE AND FITTINGS

5 Classic character ◄

Giving your bathroom a country look is partly a question of sticking to traditional style. The sleek, streamlined shapes of many contemporary fixtures tend to be intrinsically urban, and haven't the stately elegance of older designs. Big, deep bathtubs and generously cut square basins have distinctive character and an uncompromising quality that makes the whole room more interesting to furnish.

6 Freestanding furniture

If you have enough space, consider installing freestanding furniture rather than built-in fittings, to avoid the sleek luxury of the hotel look. A traditional rolltop bathtub standing in the center of the room brings its own sense of indulgence, yet takes you back to the days when this was simply a room to bathe in, so that being able to draw hot water with the turn of a faucet feels enough of a luxury without all the latest modern conveniences and spray attachments.

A big, square basin in classic white and fitted with capstan-head faucets delivers an instant sense of traditional style.

7 **Washstands and dressing tables** ▶
If you have the space, add a little dressing table, or a chest or washstand, to hold your toiletries and accessories, and suddenly the room becomes a place to display photographs and china and other personal treasures. A plain pine chest can be painted if you want a lighter, fresher effect than golden wood grain, or you could sit a slab of marble on top to improvise the look of a traditional washstand.

8 **Plain white porcelain**
Keep the fittings in classic white to ensure that the look never dates, however many times you redecorate. White is far more versatile than any of the colors with which bathroom designers have tried to woo us. It will adapt effortlessly to any color scheme and any style of furnishing and always stay crisp and clean.

A little wooden dressing table supplements windowsill shelf space by providing an extra surface for toiletries and accessories.

9 **Painted cabinets**
Bathroom cabinets can often be updated rather than having to be replaced. Fitted cabinets are sometimes designed with rather clumsy louvered slats, for instance—useful for keeping the contents aired, but uncomfortably like ventilation shaft covers, especially when stained in dark wood varnish. Give them a quick coat of green or blue paint and they instantly take on the look of Mediterranean shutters. Leave the finish slightly distressed if you want a weathered, sun-bleached effect.

10 **Cushions and comfort** ◀
The secret of making a bathroom truly inviting is to think of it as a proper room rather than a functional washing area. Soften the clinical edge by furnishing it as place where you will enjoy spending time, not somewhere you use only when you have to. Add a pretty cushion or two so that the obligatory bathroom chair actually becomes comfortable to sit on. Best of all, try to find space for a squashy armchair or elegant chaise longue, to give the impression that this is a room in which to relax—a sitting room that just happens to be equipped with bathing facilities as well.

Adding a comfortable armchair will help turn a functional bathroom into a place where you can relax and unwind.

11 Bath-side tables

Add a small side table next to the bath rather than relying on the surfaces provided by built-in furniture. It all reinforces the sense that this is a fully furnished room rather than a collection of fixtures, and it provides somewhere to keep soaps and shampoos close at hand, as well as holds brushes, mirrors, or scented pot-pourri. Natural or painted wood will match a simple seaside scheme, while decorative metalwork adds a more elegant touch.

12 Mirrors and cheval glasses ▶

Look for attractive mirrors that will increase the sense of light and space in your bathroom as well as provide beautiful features in their own right. Traditional cheval glasses, supported on a frame so the mirror can tilt to the required angle, add their own style if you have enough floor space, and smaller tabletop versions—sometimes fitted with an integral drawer—will turn a plain washstand into a charming dressing table. Choose your mirror for its frame, and don't worry too much if the glass itself is damaged or in need of resilvering: it is the shape and character that will create the strongest impact.

An interesting mirror will add decorative interest as well as serve a practical purpose and increase the light level.

ATTRACTIVE WAYS TO STORE YOUR TOWELS

● *Shelves and linen presses* A stack of freshly laundered towels gives even the simplest bathroom a sense of reassuring comfort. Keep them neatly folded on scented shelf liners, so they become a real luxury to use.

● *Pegs and hooks* Wooden peg-rails and old-fashioned coat hooks are just as useful for towels as clothes. Stitch a fabric loop into one of the longer edges of a bath towel, or into the corner of a hand towel, to make hanging easier, and fix the rail or hooks at a practical height for everyone to reach.

● *Orchard ladders* These classic designs will lean elegantly against a bathroom wall, their lower rungs wide enough to take several neatly folded towels, the upper framework tapering gracefully.

● *Towel stands* The traditional freestanding rail, with wooden bars attached to a slim arched frame at either end, makes a good display stand for attractive linens and can be positioned in front of a radiator for airing, or wherever your bathroom layout suggests a suitable space.

● *Blanket boxes* Store fresh, dry towels in a floor-standing chest or trunk, and the top will provide you with an extra surface for toiletries, a side table next to the bath or, if you add a couple of cushions, a comfortable place to sit.

● *Clotheshorses* An old-fashioned wooden clotheshorse designed to take drying laundry will also hold your bathroom linens. Like the purpose-built towel stand, it can be moved to wherever

you need it, but it has the extra bonus of folding away flat when not in use.

● *Coat stands* Where floor space is limited, amalgamate the benefits of the peg-rail and the towel stand and install a traditional coat stand or hatstand in a neat corner or behind the door, providing a cluster of hooks on which you can hang your linens. ▼

A wooden coat stand with plenty of practical hooks provides a useful place to hang bathroom towels.

13 Sloping ceilings ▶

Exploit the character and interest of attic spaces by fitting a bathroom under the roof, where the sloping ceilings and quirky angles won't interfere with the use of the room. Reserve the highest part of the space for hand basins and mirrors, where standing room is necessary, and use the low-ceilinged areas under the eaves for the bath and lavatory, or for a dressing table and chair. Highlight the idiosyncrasies of the shape by painting the ceiling a different color from the walls, or picking out beams and woodwork in a contrasting shade.

14 Wicker linen baskets

Traditional wicker has a natural place in country bathrooms, with deep hampers providing capacious storage for linen and laundry. Use old-fashioned linen baskets to hold fresh towel supplies and discarded clothing, and provide smaller baskets and woven bins, stacked under washstands on shelves, for cleaning materials and other essentials.

15 Lloyd Loom furniture

Look for traditional bathroom furniture such as old Lloyd Loom pieces, which look like painted wicker but are in fact made from woven and plaited paper reinforced by steel wire. Comfortable chairs and cushion-topped laundry baskets are classic Lloyd Loom designs, with a simple practicality that's perfect for bathrooms and a slightly faded appearance that always evokes well-worn country style.

Sloping ceilings create interesting angles, providing unusual storage slots under the eaves.

STORAGE

16 **Wall cabinets** ▶
Decorative wall cabinets and shelf units will store toiletries neatly out of the way if you are short of washstand space or other surfaces. Look for neat little Shaker-style cabinets with plain planked doors or a simple pattern cut in the front panel, or line an old cabinet with pretty wallpaper to provide a flash of color when it is opened. For a thrifty, utility feel, update an old mesh-fronted kitchen cabinet, so the colors of bath oils and crystals are visible through the wire mesh.

17 **Drawstring bags**
Keep the floor area clear by using drawstring bags hung on hooks or pegs to store things like clean facecloths, spare soaps, and absorbent cotton. Larger bags will keep laundry and children's bathing suits out of the way, and smaller ones can be appropriated as individual wash bags by each member of the family.

A glass-fronted cabinet lined with floral paper adds restrained decoration to the plain walls of a utility-style bathroom, offsetting the functional, slightly stark feel of the furnishings.

BATHROOM DETAILS TO EVOKE SEASIDE STYLE

● *Shells* Use real shells as decorations and trimmings. Alternatively, embroider shell motifs onto towels and curtains, or cut the fabric into scalloped edgings reminiscent of undulating waves.

● *Boats* Stand little model boats on shelves and washstands, and look for boat-patterned fabrics and wallpapers to decorate the room.

● *Lighthouses* Paint cabinet doors and laundry bins with images of the familiar striped towers (great for encouraging children to tidy away damp towels and dirty clothes).

● *Fish* Bright-painted wooden, ceramic, or papier-mâché fish can swim across windowsills and along the side of the bath, and nestle among towels. Look for ceramic motifs that can be stuck onto plain tiles to create an occasional relief pattern around your walls or splashback.

● *Beach pebbles* Display them in shallow dishes to enjoy their subtle, toning shades, delicate veining, and smooth, tactile shapes. Alternatively, tie a number of them securely with lengths of string to make a decorative mobile to hang from a corner of the ceiling (see tip 25 on page 132).

DETAILS AND ACCESSORIES

18 **Fresh flowers** ▶
Keep the room stocked with freshly cut flowers for scent and color so the bathroom becomes a place in which to relax and linger. Choose roses, freesias, or lilies-of-the-valley for the softest fragrance, or plant a bowl with sweet hyacinth bulbs to place on the windowsill. Borrow decorative china from other parts of the house to display the flowers and make the room feel pretty and furnished.

19 **Water pitchers**
Add an old-fashioned ewer and water basin on top of a washstand or table. Enamel will suit the functional simplicity of a utility-style room, or you could look for pretty porcelain Victoriana for a more decorative effect. The days are long gone when these were a necessity for providing hot water, but the graceful shapes still furnish modern bathrooms with a touch of classic elegance.

Fresh flowers give bathrooms a touch of luxury. Display them in pretty china, and choose blooms to match the colors of your soaps and linens.

20 Colored oils and crystals

Bathrooms are full of opportunities to add decorative color on country themes. Seek out the prettiest crystals and bath oils and line them up on shelves and windowsills where they can glow in the light. Pick soaps that match the rest of your color scheme and pile them luxuriously in baskets and dishes, ready for use.

21 Pretty soap dishes

Make use of pretty china and the natural beauty of sea shells to improvise unusual soap dishes. A stray porcelain saucer or plate from a disused or incomplete china collection will have more individual charm than a mass-produced, purpose-designed dish, and shallow, fan-shaped scallop shells will reflect the bathroom's associations with water and the sea.

22 Classic faucets ▶

Authentic country bathrooms need traditional capstan-head faucets to go with their rolltop bathtubs and big square-cornered sinks. Original faucets can be found at architectural salvage centers, although you need to check that they have been reseated to eliminate any problems of lime buildup that could cause blockages. Otherwise, look for new faucets in classic designs and finishes that suit the style of the room.

Seek out traditional-style faucets to complete your country bathroom.

23 Hidden heaters

Heating designers have come up with innumerable ideas to reinvent the radiator or disguise it. Many of the modern styles are better suited to contemporary, urban bathrooms, but you will also find heaters that can be built invisibly into the wall. Another option is to go for sleekly designed ladder radiators or heated towel rails, and then add a country touch by hanging lavender bags or pomanders from them so that the scent is stimulated by the heat.

COUNTRY STYLES FOR BATHROOM WINDOWS

● *Roman shades* Softer than a basic roller shade but less fussy than a gathered curtain, the gentle folds of the Roman shade can be arranged to form a deep valance screening the upper part of the window, or lowered completely to cover the window with a neat fabric panel.

● *Single curtain* One curtain will screen the window just as efficiently as two, and can be tied loosely in the center during the day, rather than being drawn to one side, to maintain an element of privacy.

● *Voile panels* Translucent sheer fabric is the perfect way to keep the bathroom flooded with light while screening it from the public gaze. For a designer touch, add simple patch pockets made from the same fabric and holding feathers, shells, or dried leaves to create intriguing details.

● *Frosted-glass effect* Etched and sandblasted glass can incorporate elegant patterning as well as obscure the view through the window. To achieve the same effect quickly, use frosting spray with a stencil template, or apply adhesive film printed with cut-out patterns.

● *Wooden shutters* Simple panels that slide down into a housing beneath the window or fold back on either side of it are neat and practical for small rooms where you don't want to deal with lots of fabric. ▶

Traditional wooden shutters are one of the best styles for a bathroom window, functional yet elegant and adding a strong sense of tradition.

24 Simple accessories

Fill the room with natural accessories that rustle up a sense of simple country living. Natural sponges and pure-bristle nail, back, and cleaning brushes supply mellow neutral colors and intriguing texture, as well as rustic authenticity. Look for plain wooden handles and bath racks, and combine them with old-fashioned tinware and enamel for an understated look of utility and practicality.

25 Beachcombing finds ◄

Create a bathroom mobile by hanging smooth pebbles or shells from a rope-bound frame. To make the frame, bend a length of stiff wire into a circle and wind soft, pliable hemp around it until the metal is completely hidden. Cut three more lengths of rope and plait them to form a hanging cord, leaving about 10–12inches (25–30cm) of the lower ends unplaited so you can tie the three ropes onto the wire ring, spacing them at regular intervals. Use finer string or twine to tie or thread your chosen pebbles or shells onto the ring, mixing different sizes and different lengths of string to form an interesting pattern. Hook the plaited rope to the ceiling so the mobile hangs freely, shifting its shape as it turns.

26 Well-stocked bookshelves

Make sure there is plenty of reading material to entertain you while you take a leisurely bath. Add a wall-mounted or floor-standing bookshelf or line up a set of favorite volumes between bookends on a windowsill, and provide baskets of magazines as though preparing a guest bedroom for a visitor.

27 Natural soaps

Enjoy the authenticity of old-fashioned soaps. Handmade olive oil soaps scented with delicious country fragrances such as rose, geranium, rosemary, honey, and lavender are available from good natural suppliers (so you don't need to go to the trouble of making your own) and come in pleasingly chunky square blocks, emphasizing their utilitarian character. Shallow terra-cotta pots, saucers, and planters borrowed from the garden will provide robust soap dishes as an alternative to delicate china.

28 Relax under drapes

Indulge in a little simple luxury by dressing the bath with flowing drapes so that it feels more like a four-poster bed. This effect works best with a freestanding bath tub that can take center stage in the style of a throne, but can also be achieved over a bath tub installed against one wall. Fix a circular shower curtain fitting above it and hang from it tab-top, tie-top, or clipped-on curtains that can enclose the bath as they drape generously around it.

29 Candles and lanterns

Lamplight and candles recreate something of the feel of the old-fashioned bathroom, before recessed spotlights took over. For real romance, indulge in the occasional candlelit bath, using glass-sided lanterns and traditional candlesticks. Set little tealights on plates, or drop them inside colored tumblers and jars to create a Christmas tree-light effect.

A mobile made of pretty shells hung from a rope-bound frame creates an intriguing silhouette against a bathroom wall.

CHAPTER EIGHT

Quick Country Essentials

Every country decorator needs a store cupboard of "decorating ingredients" that can be used to create instant effects whenever they're needed, transforming anything from floors and walls to windows and accessories. This chapter is a sourcebook of ideas to supplement the preceding room-by-room coverage—a treasure chest of things to look out for and hold on to, with quick ideas for how and where to use them, ranging from offcuts and leftovers from previous projects, to finds brought home after beachcombing and hedgerow walks.

PAINT

1 Tester pots
Never throw away tester pots and leftovers: small quantities can go a long way in decorative projects. Just keep the tins well sealed in a cool, dry place and stir the paint well before using it.

2 Hand-painted patterns
Use painted patterns to create your own designs on plain parchment lampshades and handmade covers for books and photograph albums. Either create freehand designs or use a stencil.

3 Furniture transformations ▼
Use latex or eggshell paint to transform small pieces of junk-store furniture and shabby old pine. Sand the wood first to give it a surface suitable for painting. If using latex, you may want to add an extra coat of wax or varnish to protect the surface.

4 Frames and accessories
Small accessories such as picture and mirror frames can be painted—and repainted—to coordinate with your furnishings, however frequently you change them.

5 Stamps and stencils
Decorate plain furniture or wall surfaces by printing or stenciling designs onto them. Stamps can be cut from linoleum, potatoes, or rubber, with stencil templates available in waxed paper or acrylic, and only a small amount of paint is needed for the pattern to be transferred onto your surface.

6 Plaques and signposts
Paint little wooden plaques to identify children's bedrooms, or to let visitors know where you are: "In the garden," or "Gone for a walk."

Paint is one of the quickest and most satisfying ways to change the look of a room.

Plain wooden chairs acquire a new identity when painted in fresh colors—perfect for country kitchens and seaside-style bathrooms.

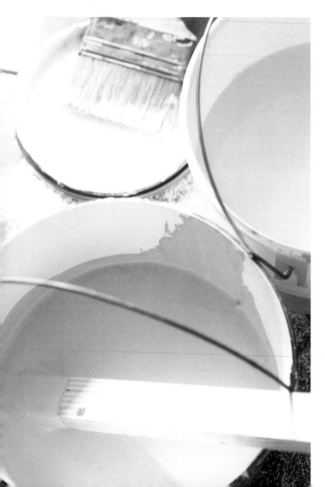

FABRIC AND RIBBON

7 Scraps and patches ▼

Keep your sewing box stocked with fabric scraps and accessories from notions stores. Favorite old clothes can be useful, too—cottons are ideal for cushion covers

and lightweight curtains, and the sound parts can be stitched into patchworks even if the actual garment is way beyond repair. Even the smallest pieces can come in handy: as long as the fabrics have roughly equal weight and strength, you can cut remnants into neat patches and stitch them together to make patchwork drapes and bedcovers.

8 Chair covers

Keep any larger pieces of fabric to make slipcovers for chairs. Carefully measure the chair section by section and cut individual lengths of fabric to fit each

Left: Fabric scraps from dressmaking projects can be used to trim furnishings and accessories.

one (remembering to add seam allowances), then stitch the whole cover together.

9 Lightweight curtains

Small windows don't take much fabric, so use leftover fabric to make simple gathered curtains and plain roller or Roman shades. Dress material is just as good as furnishing fabric for lightweight drapes.

10 Simple cushions ▼

Stitch simple cushion covers in contrasting fabrics, or use matching fabric to turn a jumble of junk-store chairs into a coordinating set.

Short lengths of fabric are perfect for cutting up to make patchworks, panels, and cushion covers.

11 **Napkins and placemats** ▼
Plain linen or printed cotton will make simple table napkins, placemats, and tray covers. Cut them into squares (for napkins) or rectangles (large enough to take a dinner plate) and turn the raw edges under, topstitching to create neat hems on all sides.

12 **Homemade lampshades**
Fit fabric around metal lampshade frames to design shades in different styles. Loosely gathered fabric will give a pretty, ruffled effect, while stretching it tightly around the frame provides a neat, tailored look. Shades can also be created by winding a length of ribbon around the frame, binding it vertically until the structure is completely covered.

Save remnants of bright cotton to make into cheerful table napkins and placemats.

13 **Greeting cards and gift tags**
Keep spare ribbon and embroidery thread to make cards and gift tags. Punch a hole through the tag and thread the cord through it, or tie it into a small bow and stick onto a piece of stiff folded cardboard.

14 **Herb pillows**
Keep a few of the prettiest scraps to make lavender bags and little herb pillows, scenting your bedroom closets and linens, and helping you sleep. Trim them with braid, lace, or ribbon from your notions hoard.

15 **Framed panels**
Frame small panels of bright fabric to hang on the wall, turning under the edges to neaten them, then mounting them on a white or colored cardboard background to make instant pictures.

16 **Jelly-jars**
Cut circular pieces to make gathered covers for jellies and preserves. Use pinking shears so that the edges won't fray, and tie them over the sealed pot with ribbon or raffia.

17 **Milk-pitcher covers**
Use napkins, handkerchiefs, and squares of decorative lace to make old-fashioned covers for small milk pitchers. Hem the edges if necessary, and trim with beads or shells to weight them.

18 **Drape headings**
Short strips of ribbon will instantly turn lightweight fabric panels into tie-top drapes. Stitch them to the top of the drape through the center of the ribbon to leave two loose ends, and tie these around the rod or wire.

19 **Shoe bags and toy bags**
Kitchen linens such as dish towels are the perfect size to turn into drawstring laundry or toy bags. Fold them in half to make flap-over envelope-style shoe bags.

20 **Ribbon ties** ▼
Use ribbon to fasten cushions (by stitching strips onto both sides of the opening and tying them in bows once the cushion pad is inside) and headboard covers (slot the cover over the board, and tie the ribbons together at either side for a decorative finish).

Reels of ribbon neatly stored are invaluable for trimming cushions, curtains, and other accessories.

PAPER

21 Drawer liners
Use sheets of paper to line the bases of drawers and shelves, helping to keep the contents clean and dust-free. Improvise the scented style of store-bought drawer liners by adding a little homemade sachet of potpourri or a wand of dried lavender flowers.

22 Door panels
Cut rectangles of wallpaper to fit the panels of an old-fashioned door, slotting the paper into the panel recesses to provide contrasting pattern against the plain paintwork of the door.

23 Boxes and files
Use offcuts of decorative paper to cover storage boxes, files, and notebooks, keeping studies and work areas looking prettier, less officelike, and generally more inviting.

Keep wallpaper remnants and giftwrap, and the tissue paper that packs expensive clothes and furnishing accessories, for use in future projects.

24 Cabinet fronts

Fix panels of floral paper behind chicken-wire cabinet fronts, providing decorative doors with a garden-style trelliswork design.

25 Cabinet linings ◄

Line the backs of cabinet interiors so you get a flash of color and pattern when the door is opened. This works particularly well in small wall-mounted cupboards such as bathroom cabinets, and in display cabinets where the paper is visible through the glass. It also makes an attractive backing for china and glass displayed on open shelves.

26 Framed papers ►

Frame panels of patterned paper as pictures to hang on the walls, using the technique described in tip 15 on page 138. Group several of these together in matching frames so they work as a complete set—perhaps juxtaposing the same pattern in different colors if you have a wallpaper book that provides samples in contrasting colors.

27 Picture borders

Use patterned paper to create borders for simple pictures, in the style of traditional marbled papers. Mount the picture on a sheet of plain white or colored paper, then cut a four-sided border (either in a single piece, or as four strips with

Left: A wall cabinet lined with decorative paper provides an elegant setting for well-chosen china.

mitered corners) to frame the mount before fitting the whole thing in a proper wooden or metal frame.

28 Homemade greetings cards

Use small sections of pattern to design your own birthday, thank-you, and special-occasion cards. Fold a piece of thin, stiff cardboard or thick watercolor paper into two, and mount a square of decorative paper on the front. Or use a few sheets of tissue and thin giftwrap, layered on top of one another in different sizes or at different angles, to create a delicate, translucent effect against the background cardboard.

29 Kitchen and study labels

Keep a supply of old-fashioned luggage labels for identifying the contents of preserve jars or files in the study. Inscribe them with an elegant calligraphy pen, or with gold or silver ink for special effects.

Sections of wallpaper, mounted and framed like paintings, make an unusual picture display against a plain wall.

CERAMICS

30 Pottery oddments
Don't get rid of oddments just because they aren't part of a matching set. Pretty china and leftover tiles can have all kinds of decorative and practical uses, so keep them safe until an opportunity arises.

31 Jugs and mugs
Borrow elegant cream jugs and pretty kitchen mugs to hold toothbrushes in the bathroom and makeup brushes in the bedroom, and to keep your supply of pens and pencils tidy in the study.

32 Soap dishes ▼
Spare saucers and plates make perfect soap dishes. Keep the more delicate designs for the bathroom, where their pretty colors and patterns will match fabrics and wallpapers, and use chunky earthenware beside the sink in mellow farmhouse-style kitchens, echoing the pieces displayed on hutches and shelves.

33 Trinket bowls
Deeper dishes and sugar bowls are even more versatile as they can also be used as dressing table containers for jewelry, makeup, and potpourri.

34 Flower holders ▶
Look for interesting containers in which to display flowers. Teapots, coffee pots, and milk pitchers are just as useful as purpose-designed vases, while miniature posies can be arranged in holders as small as mustard pots and eggcups.

35 Display pieces
Don't discard a piece of china just because it is cracked or chipped. It may no longer be suitable for holding liquids or for everyday handling, but it can still be used to display dried flowers and grasses, and will still look beautiful standing on a shelf or tabletop. (Just remember to be careful how you pick it up, avoiding stress on mended handles and other cracks.)

Left: Pretty kitchen or dining room ceramics can be requisitioned as potpourri holders and soap dishes.
Right: An elegant cup and saucer make an inpromptu vase for a posy of freshly cut garden roses.

36 Utensil stands
Heavy pitchers can be deployed to hold utensils on a kitchen worktop. Use them for wooden spoons, rolling pins, whisks, and spatulas—anything that is too long or cumbersome for a drawer and that you want to keep easily accessible.

37 Mosaics ◄
Broken china and cracked tiles are an invaluable source of materials for making mosaics. Tabletops, flowerpots, plain ceramics, and sections of wall can all be decorated with chips of plain or patterned color to create your own designs. Spread the surface with ceramic adhesive, then press the mosaic pieces into place. Once it is dry, you can grout around the design, wiping the excess away with a damp cloth.

38 Decorative splashbacks
If you have a few decorative tiles left over from decorating projects, that's probably enough to make a splashback. A small sink may only need three or four to line the wall behind it, while, for a larger area, you can insert them among a run of plain tiles to add a touch of pattern.

39 Tile tablemats
Individual tiles can be used as heat-resistant table mats and coffeepot stands if you back them with felt to prevent them from scratching polished surfaces.

Colored fragments of old china or ceramic tile can be used to decorate larger ceramics in a random mosaic effect.

GLASS

40 Tealight lanterns
Every country kitchen should have a supply of empty jelly jars. Turn them into lanterns by standing a little tealight inside each one and twisting a length of wire handle around the rim to make a handle.

41 Recycled jars
Collect Mason jars of all shapes and make your own jams, jellies, preserves, and sauces to stock your pantry. Bottle your own fruit, pickle spare vegetables, and create colorful chutneys to line up along kitchen shelves.

42 Interesting bottles ▶
Look out for interesting bottles to display in their own right or to fill with home-flavored oils and vinegars. Stand them against a window so that the light glows through the natural colors.

43 Chips and fragments
Even fragments of broken glass, as long as they have no sharp or jagged edges, are worth keeping for decoration. Pebble-smooth pieces, sea-washed and frosted in appearance, can be collected on beach walks and displayed in a pretty dish, while larger chunks, if their edges are polished, can be set on the sill or frame of a window to catch the light like an ornamental crystal.

Old bottles, complete with their spring-release stoppers, can be lined up along a windowsill or used to hold homemade oils and vinegars.

BUTTONS AND BEADS

44 Domestic treasures

As well as the more usual sewing-box accessories, keep broken jewelry so you can put individual gems to new ornamental use. This will become the country decorator's treasure chest, a hoard of many-colored baubles that add a touch of magic to plain surfaces.

45 Colored droplets

Use colored beads to create a rainbow of droplets catching the light from lampshades and chandeliers. Stitch them around the rim of the shade, or hang them from the chandelier arms so that they swing and turn.

46 Button-trimmed lampshades ◄

Decorate a simple linen or paper lampshade with buttons, either fixing them in vertical stripes or horizontal bands to create a pattern, or covering the whole shade so it acquires a decorative shell.

47 Buttoned-up bed linen

Use buttons to fasten pillowcases and duvet covers too. Look in notions stores for old-fashioned linen-covered buttons for a practical, fresh-from-the-laundry finish, or choose decorative, contrasting designs that stand out against the plain white cotton of the bed linen.

48 Button-top curtains

Buttons always give simple curtains a neat, tailored look. Use them to finish a row of fabric tabs along the top, or to attach a lining to the main curtain, or just for effect, to provide a smart edging.

49 Decorative cushions ▶

Stitch a row of buttons along a cushion opening to act as a fastening instead of a zipper, or trim the edges with decorative beads for ornament and color.

A plain lampshade covered with small matching buttons in a repeating pattern acquires a neat, thrifty appeal.

Panels of plain color are decorated with a sprinkling of tiny beads and smart buttoned corners to make an elegant cushion cover.

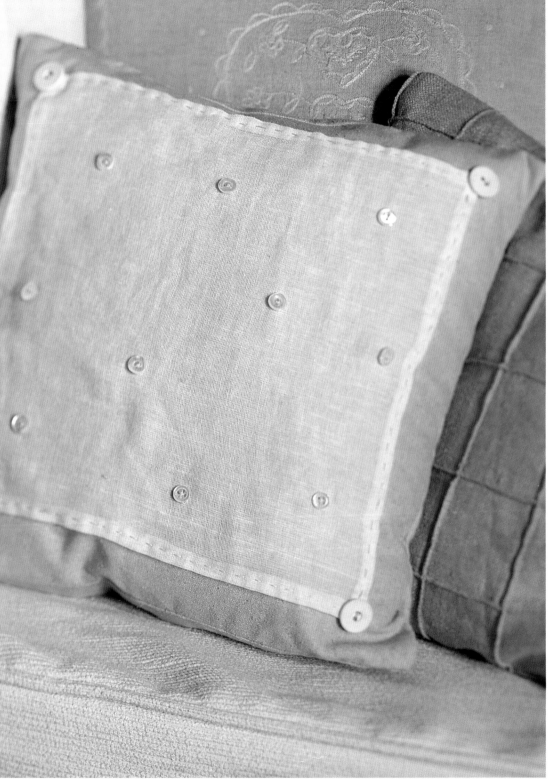

50 Beaded table linen
Stitch buttons and beads onto plain table linen, to give your dining room an extra sparkle. Napkins can be trimmed with a border of buttons, or rolled into a buttoned cuff instead of a conventional ring, while an edging of colored beads will help to weight your tablecloth in place as well as add decoration. Weighting smaller pieces of fabric will create neat food or milk-pitcher covers (see tip 17 on page 138).

51 Mother-of-pearl gift tags ▼
Design your own homemade cards and gift tags, stitching a simple button, or a row of two or three, onto a plain luggage label, or using a cluster of tiny mother-of-pearl buttons to create a delicate pattern.

Below: A cluster of buttons decorates a plain brown luggage tag, turning it into a pretty gift card.

GARDEN SUPPLIES

52 Garden tools ◄
The garden shed is a mine of
intriguing ingredients that bring a natural
robustness to your decorating plans. Enjoy
the worn handles and intricate metal parts
of traditional garden tools, keeping them
just for display, or turning them into
practical items such as door knockers
and wall hooks.

53 Flowerpots
Terra-cotta flowerpots make
brilliant candleholders (either for single
candles or clusters of tapers) and gift
baskets. Fill them with bulbs and seeds
for a gardening present, or with soaps,
scents, and bunches of lavender to make
a collection of bathroom treats.

54 Metal buckets
Old-fashioned metal buckets can
be turned into umbrella stands, trash cans,
and office storage containers—and also
make rustic flower holders for simple
arrangements of garden blooms and
hedgerow foliage. Think of flowers on sale
at a market stall, and mass bunches of
tulips, chrysanthemums, or big mop-head
hydrangeas for a stunning display.

Put beautiful old tools and watering cans on show, and
use terra-cotta flowerpots as candleholders and
gift containers.

55 Garden twine

Soft garden twine in natural hemp color or restful green is invaluable stuff. Use it to bind lamp bases and tumblers to give them a rustic finish, and to wrap country-style presents and attach home-made gift tags.

56 Trugs and baskets ▶

Keep a stack of trugs and baskets for additional storage throughout the house. They will hold vegetables in the kitchen, toiletries in the bathroom, papers and magazines in the study, and shoes and gloves in the hall.

57 Chicken-wire

Rolls of chicken-wire have decorative uses as well as practical. Cut panels of trellis-patterned wire to front cabinet doors (with or without a backing of decorative fabric or paper). Keep smaller sections to slot into the necks of vases to hold flowers and foliage upright.

Traditional woven baskets have innumerable uses for simple storage in kitchens, bathrooms, bedrooms, and studies.

NATURAL FINDS

58 Leaves

Dry the most beautiful leaves you can find to preserve their elegant shapes and use them to bring the hedgerow into your home—adding them to displays of fresh flowers and foliage, clipping them onto curtain headings, and pressing them onto book covers and storage boxes. The most traditional of country ingredients, these simple accessories have unbeatable charm that reflects the changing seasons in your furnishings.

59 Feathers

Pick up elegantly marked feathers, keeping the stiffer spines to stand in a vase or create a plumed lampshade, and reserving softer, more delicate feathers to display within translucent pockets in sheer voile or cheesecloth curtains.

60 Shells ◄

Look for shells in delicate colors and pretty shapes to decorate bathrooms and bedrooms. Display them on shelves or massed in little dishes, and use them to make pictures and gift tags, to decorate picture and mirror frames, and to trim cushions and curtains.

Traditional country finds such as shells, feathers, and foliage are perfect ingredients for making a ceiling-hung mobile.

61 Twigs and bark

Tie crisp twigs into bundles to hang from mobiles and wreaths. Mix with dark green foliage to surround candles for wintry table decorations. Cut longer pieces into equal lengths to cover a lamp base.

62 Fir cones

Use the neat, ridged shapes of fir cones in simple table displays and to give definition to wreaths and mobiles. Pile them in baskets and dishes, and use them to fill empty fireplace grates during summer.

63 Stones and pebbles

Make use of large pebbles as paperweights in your study, or incorporate them into dining room place settings, painting them with guests' names and arranging one on each plate.

64 Grasses and foliage

Collect grasses and rushes as well as flowers and foliage, creating dramatic arrangements in tall vases and using the dried seed coats in wreaths, centerpieces, and other decorations.

65 Fresh flowers ▶

Enjoy the scent and color of fresh flowers throughout the year, and press or dry a selection of them to use in decorative projects such as making potpourri, home-made pictures, and papier-mâché designs.

Delicate flowers can be displayed in fresh arrangements, or dried and used in other decorations around the home.

PHOTOGRAPHIC ACKNOWLEDGMENTS

Caroline Arber pages 14 (top), 21, 36, 37, 42, 60 (right), 94, 95, 112, 132, 138 (left), 143
Jan Baldwin pages 106, 110
Adrian Briscoe pages 7, 52, 55, 57 (right), 61, 115
Charlie Colmer pages 4, 72, 9, 14 (bottom), 19, 23 (top), 24, 54, 71, 73, 76, 84, 107, 108, 109, 134, 137 (bottom), 141, 145
Harry Cory Wright page 93
Christopher Drake pages 40, 47, 90, 120, 126, 130, 139, 142
Chrysalis Images pages 29, 75, 147 (left)
Tim Evan-Cook page 91
Kate Gadsby pages 63, 96, 121 (top), 144, 148
David George page 136 (right)
Catherine Gratwicke pages 18, 26, 28, 30, 43, 50, 53, 56, 68, 77, 103, 128, 136 (left), 140, 146, 147 (right), 150
Johnathon Gregson page 62
Huntley Hedworth pages 25, 98, 122
David Hiscock pages 60 (middle), 82, 97, 111
Tom Leighton pages 12, 32, 33, 74, 89

Mark Luscombe-Whyte pages 13, 102
James Merrell pages 10, 15, 17, 27, 34, 39, 41, 58, 78, 80, 85, 86, 87, 104, 105, 118, 121 (bottom), 124, 125, 151
Alex Ramsay page 69
Trevor Richards pages 38, 70, 116, 119
Tham Nhu Tran pages 2, 22, 48, 57 (left), 72, 88 (both), 99, 123, 127, 129, 131, 137 (top), 149
Debi Treloar pages 35, 45, 67, 92, 100, 113
Pia Tryde pages 20 (both), 59, 64, 138 (right)
Peter Woloszynski pages 16, 114
Polly Wreford pages 23, 51, 60 (left)
Simon Upton page 66

Styling by: Ben Kendrick, Kristin Perers, Pippa Rimmer, Sophie Martell, Hester Page, Laura Vine, Gabi Tubbs, Katrin Cargill, Carolyn Bailey, Jayne Keeley, Nicola Goodwin, Mary Norden, Hans Blomquist, Jemima Mills, Margaret Caselton, Caroline Zoob, Helen Bratby, Julia Bird.